AF455220

CONTENTS

INTRODUCTION
ESSENTIALS OF POWERXL AIR FRYER GRILL

What is the PowerXL Air Fryer Grill?

A multifunction air fryer and grill, the PowerXL Air Fryer Grill offers a plethora of menu possibilities with up to 70 percent fewer calories from fat than traditional frying.

It features eight cooking presets that let you air fry and grill at the same time, air fry, grill, toast, broil, rotisserie or reheat food with less cooking oil or none at all. It also does not require thawing and can cook food straight from the freezer.

The PowerXL Air Fryer Grill boasts an up to 450-degree superheated air circulation that ensures the food is cooked evenly on all sides, extra crispy on the outside and tenderly juicy on the inside.

The unit heats almost instantly with a smart preheat feature that starts the timer only when it reaches the desired temperature. It also shuts off automatically.

Equipped with two racks, the PowerXL Air Fryer Grill can cook as much as 4.5 times more food than traditionally smaller air fryers. Ideal for cooking meals for the whole family or when hosting a gathering, the large capacity allows the unit to accommodate up to 10 pounds of chicken, a 12-inch round pizza, six toast slices or bagels, or the equivalent load of a 4.5-quart Dutch oven.

The Working Principle

In general, air fryers feature a fan that circulates hot air within its chambers in order to cook food. The hot air radiates from the chamber through the heating elements near the food.

To control the temperature, excess hot air is released through an air inlet on the top and an exhaust at the back of the unit.

Instead of being completely submerged in hot oil, food in air fryers are air-heated to induce the Maillard reaction, resulting in browned food with a distinct aroma and taste.

The PowerXL Air Fryer Grill's fan is equipped with turbo blades that are more powerful than its competitors. These blades are angled strategically in order to distribute heat evenly over the surface of the food. Depending on the kind of food, cooking times are reduced by at least 20 percent in comparison with that of traditional ovens.

It also comes with a non-stick grill plate that creates gorgeous grill marks and chargrill flavor without the use of charcoal or propane.

Step-by-step Procedure of Using It

Operating your PowerXL Air Fryer Grill is a breeze with its easy to assemble parts and accessories and simple control panel. After choosing the desired settings, you can just leave it and forget about it until it is time to eat.

Before using the unit for the first time, read all materials, labels and stickers. Remove all packaging, labels and stickers prior to operation. Hand wash all removable parts and accessories with soapy water.

Place the PowerXL Air Fryer Grill on a safe, stable, level, horizontal and heat-resistant surface in an area with good air circulation. Keep the unit away from hot surfaces, other objects or appliances, and combustible materials. It is advisable to plug the unit to a designated outlet.

Carefully assemble the parts and accessories. On the left side of the air fryer's door, you will see guides that indicate the ideal place for the racks and pans. The drip tray should be kept below the heating elements at all times when cooking.
Preheat the unit to allow the manufacturer's protective coating to burn, and then wipe off with a warm moist cloth.
Lightly grease the food before cooking to ensure that it would not stick to the pan or to each other. You may opt to use healthier plant-based oils like avocado and olive. If you are cooking wet food such as marinated meat, pat them dry first to avoid excessive splattering and smoke while cooking.
Avoid overcrowding the food for hot air to circulate effectively and achieve crispy results. Also keep in mind that air fryers cook food faster so follow recommended temperature settings to avoid overcooking or burning.
There are three knobs for: (1)adjusting temperature(up to 450 degrees)and toast darkness options, (2)selecting cooking function (air fry, air fry/grill, grill, broil, pizza/bake, reheat, toast/bagel, rotisserie), and setting the timer(up to 120 minutes).
To make toast, set the toast darkness first and then choose the toast/bagel function. Next, turn the timer knob clockwise past the 20-minute mark, and then rotate counterclockwise to the toast icon.
For the rest of the cooking functions, turn the timer knob past the 20-minute mark before adjusting it to the desired time.
You must select a cooking function for the device to start. When a cooking function and time have been set, the light will turn on. Once the timer expires, the light goes off.

Tips for Care & Maintenance

It is a good practice to visually inspect your PowerXL Air Fryer before each use to make sure that it will function safely and properly. Air fryers may be built to last a long time but just like any other kitchen appliance, you may encounter a few minor and easy-to-fix problems with them from time to time.

Cleaning & Deodorizing

Make sure that the unit is clean before each use. Check the inside for any debris or accumulated dust if you have not been using your unit for some time.

Clean the unit immediately after each use, especially after cooking foods with a pungent smell. Unplug the air fryer and allow it to cool down for at least 30 minutes.

All of the removable parts and accessories are dishwasher safe. If you prefer to handwash, use a mild detergent and soft moist cloth. Do not use abrasive cleaning materials.

Regularly empty the accumulated fat from the bottom of the machine to avoid excessive smoke when cooking.

How to Store It

After cleaning, make sure that the unit and all its parts and components are dry before storing away. Ensure that the unit will be kept in a stable, level and upright position while in storage. Keep it in a cool, dry place.

Frequently Asked Questions (FAQs)

What is unit size and load capacity of the PowerXL Air Fryer Grill?

The product measures 15.1 x 19.3 x 10. 4 inches, with a capacity of 930 cubic inches.

What is the wattage?

1500 watts

What are the accessories that come with the Air Fryer Grill?

The PowerXL Air Fryer Grill has a grill plate, crisper tray, a rotisserie spit set, a baking pan, a drip tray, and an oven/pizza rack. The deluxe unit also includes a non-stick griddle plate and an egg/muffin tray.

Will the PowerXL Air Fryer Grill help me eat healthier?

The PowerXL Air Fryer Grill uses hot air instead of oil or butter to produce browned and crispy results, creating lower-calorie alternative versions of our favorite deep-fried foods.

What food can I cook in the PowerXL Air Fryer grill?

You can crisp anything from roasted chicken and steak to potatoes and vegetables. The eight cooking functions can assure you that whether craving classic French fries or corn muffins, your all-in-one air fryer got it all for you.

BREAKFAST AND BRUNCH RECIPES

Breakfast Sausage Patties

Servings: 4

Cooking Time: 10 Minutes

Ingredients:

- Cooking spray
- 12 oz. sausage patties
- 4 slices whole wheat bread

Directions:

1. Preheat your air fryer to 400 degrees F.
2. Spray sausage patties with oil.
3. Add the sausage patties to the air fryer rack.
4. Cook for 5 minutes per side.
5. Serve with whole wheat bread slices.

Two Ingredient Cream Biscuit R

Servings: 4-6

Cooking Time: 15 Mins

Ingredients:

- 2 cups self-rising flour
- 1 1/2 cups heavy whipping cream

Directions:

1. Preheat oven to 475º F. Lightly coat rimmed baking sheet or cast iron skillet with vegetable shortening. Set aside.
2. Add flour to a large mixing bowl. Slowly pour in heavy whipping cream and stir gently until just combined. Do not over mix.
3. Pour biscuit dough onto a floured countertop or dough board. Gently pat or roll to about 1/2-inch thick. Cut out biscuits using about a 2-inch biscuit cutter. Place biscuits into skillet or on baking sheet pan, leaving about an inch between biscuits to allow them to rise and cook fully. Place in preheated oven and bake about 10-12 minutes. Remove from oven and serve.

Nutrition Info: Calories: 355kcal, Carbohydrates: 31g, Protein: 6g, Fat: 22g, Saturated Fat: 13g, Cholesterol: 81mg, Sodium: 23mg, Potassium: 86mg

Sausage Omelet

Servings: 2

Cooking Time: 23 Minutes

Ingredients:

- 2 sausage, chopped
- 1 yellow onion
- 1 bacon slice
- 4 eggs

Directions:

1. Preheat the PowerXL Air Fryer Grill by selecting air fry mode
2. Adjust temperature to 320°F and time to 5 minutes
3. In a bowl, mix all the ingredients.
4. Pour into the air fryer baking tray
5. Transfer into the PowerXL Air Fryer Grill
6. Air fry for 10 minutes
7. Serve and enjoy!

Nutrition Info: Calories: 156kcal, Fat: 21g, Carb: 27g, Proteins: 17g

Air Fryer Grilled Cheese

Servings: 1 sandwich

Cooking Time: 8 Mins

Ingredients:

- 2 slices bread
- 1/2 cup shredded cheese such as fontina, cheddar, gouda, muenster
- 1 tbsp room temperature salted butter divided

Directions:

1. Stack cheese between two slices of bread then butter the exterior of the sandwich.
2. Place buttered grilled cheese in air fryer basket and set the temperature for 370F degrees for 4 minutes.
3. When the timer has gone off, flip it and put it back in for 3 more minutes at 370F degrees.
4. Carefully remove from air fryer basket, slice in half and serve immediately.

Nutrition Info: Calories: 330 Fat 19g Satfat 6g Unsatfat 10g Protein 23g Carbohydrate 9g Fiber 3g Sugars 2g

Pepperoni Omelet

Servings: 2

Cooking Time: 25 Minutes

Ingredients:

- 2 tbsp. milk
- 4 eggs
- 10 pepperoni slices
- Salt and ground black pepper to taste

Directions:

1. Preheat the PowerXL Air Fryer Grill by selecting air fry mode
2. Adjust temperature to 350°F and time to 5 minutes
3. In a bowl, mix all the ingredients.
4. Pour into the Air fryer baking tray
5. Transfer into the PowerXL Air Fryer Grill
6. Air fry for 12 minutes
7. Serve and enjoy!

Nutrition Info: Calories: kcal, Fat: g, Carb: g, Proteins: g

Spinach And Bacon Muffins

Servings: 4

Cooking Time: 10 Minutes

Ingredients:

- 2 strips turkey bacon, cut in half crosswise
- 2 whole-grain English muffins, split
- 1 cup fresh baby spinach, long stems removed
- ¼ ripe pear, peeled and thinly sliced
- 4 slices Provolone cheese

Directions:

1. Put the turkey bacon strips in the air fryer basket.
2. Place the basket on the air fry position.
3. Select Air Fry, set temperature to 390ºF (199ºC), and set time to 6 minutes. Flip the strips halfway through the cooking time.
4. When cooking is complete, the bacon should be crisp.
5. Remove from the air fryer grill and drain on paper towels. Set aside.
6. Put the muffin halves in the air fryer basket.
7. Select Air Fry and set time to 2 minutes. Return the basket to the air fryer grill. When done, the muffin halves will be lightly browned.
8. Remove the basket from the air fryer grill. Top each muffin half with ¼ of the baby spinach, several pear slices, a strip of turkey bacon, followed by a slice of cheese.
9. Select Bake, set temperature to 360ºF (182ºC), and set time to 2 minutes. Place the basket back to the air fryer grill. When done, the cheese will be melted.
10. Serve warm.

Bacon, Egg And Cheese Breakfast Hash

Servings: 4

Cooking Time: 35 Minutes

Ingredients:

- 2 slices of bacon
- 4 tiny potatoes
- 1/4 tomato
- 1 egg
- 1/4 cup of shredded cheese

Directions:

1. Preheat the PowerXL Air Fryer Grill to 200ºC or 400ºF on bake mode. Set bits of bacon on a double-layer tin foil.
2. Cut the vegetables to put over the bacon. Crack an egg over it.
3. Shape the tin foil into a bowl and cook it in the PowerXL Air Fryer Grill at 177ºC or 350ºF for 15-20 minutes. Put some shredded cheese on top.

Nutrition Info: Calories: 150.5 kcal, Carbs: 18g, Protein: 6g, Fat: 6g.

Crispy Sweet Potato Chips

Servings: 6 To 8 Slices

Cooking Time: 8 Minutes

Ingredients:

- 1 small sweet potato, cut into ⅜ inch-thick slices
- 2 tablespoons olive oil
- 1 to 2 teaspoon ground cinnamon

Directions:

1. Add the sweet potato slices and olive oil in a bowl and toss to coat. Fold in the cinnamon and stir to combine.
2. Lay the sweet potato slices in a single layer in the air fryer basket.
3. Place the basket on the air fry position.
4. Select Air Fry, set temperature to 390ºF (199ºC), and set time to 8 minutes. Stir the potato slices halfway through the cooking time.
5. When cooking is complete, the chips should be crisp. Remove the basket from the air fryer grill. Allow to cool for 5 minutes before serving.

Bacon & Eggs

Servings: 4

Cooking Time: 16 Minutes

Ingredients:

- 8 slices bacon
- 4 sunny side up eggs
- 2 cups avocado, sliced into cubes

Directions:

1. Select air fry function.
2. Preheat your air fryer to 390 degrees F.
3. Add the bacon slices to the air fryer rack.
4. Air fry for 8 minutes per side.
5. Serve crispy bacon strips with eggs and avocado.

Easy Cinnamon Rolls

Servings: 18 Rolls

Cooking Time: 25 Minutes

Ingredients:

- $^1/_3$ cup light brown sugar
- 2 teaspoons cinnamon
- All-purpose flour, for dusting
- 1 (9-by-9-inch) frozen puff pastry sheet, thawed
- 6 teaspoons unsalted butter, melted, divided

Directions:

1. In a small bowl, stir together the brown sugar and cinnamon.
2. On a clean work surface, lightly dust with the flour and lay the puff pastry sheet. Using a rolling pin, press the folds together and roll the dough out in one direction so that it measures about 9 by 11 inches. Cut it in half to form two squat rectangles of about 5½ by 9 inches.
3. Brush 2 teaspoons of the butter over each pastry half. Sprinkle with 2 tablespoons of the cinnamon sugar. Pat it down lightly with the palm of your hand to help it adhere to the butter.
4. Starting with the 9-inch side of one rectangle. Using your hands, carefully roll the dough into a cylinder. Repeat with the other rectangle. To make slicing easier, refrigerate the rolls for 10 to 20 minutes.
5. Using a sharp knife, slice each roll into nine 1-inch pieces. Transfer the rolls to the center of the sheet pan. They should be very close to each other, but not quite touching. Drizzle the remaining 2 teaspoons of the butter over the rolls and sprinkle with the remaining cinnamon sugar.
6. Place the pan on the bake position.
7. Select Bake, set temperature to 350ºF (180ºC) and set time to 25 minutes.
8. When cooking is complete, remove the pan and check the rolls. They should be puffed up and golden brown.
9. Let the rolls rest for 5 minutes and transfer them to a wire rack to cool completely. Serve.

Bagel

Servings: 4

Cooking Time: 15 Minutes

Ingredients:

- 1 cup all purpose flour
- 2 teaspoons baking powder
- ½ teaspoon salt
- 1 cup nonfat Greek yogurt
- 1 egg, beaten

Directions:

1. In a bowl, mix all the ingredients.
2. Knead the mixture.
3. Divide the dough into 4.
4. Roll into a thick rope and then form a bagel.
5. Brush the top with egg.
6. Choose bake setting in the air fryer grill.
7. Set it to 280 degrees F.
8. Cook for 15 minutes.

Scrambled Egg

Servings: 1

Cooking Time: 20 Minutes

Ingredients:

- 2 eggs
- 2 tbsp. Butter
- 1/4 cup of cheese
- 1 tomato

Directions:

1. Preheat the PowerXL Air Fryer Grill by selecting air fry mode
2. Adjust temperature to 290°F and time to 5 minutes
3. Grease the baking tray with the butter.
4. In a bowl, mix all the ingredients.
5. Pour into the Air fryer baking tray
6. Transfer into the PowerXL Air Fryer Grill
7. Air fry for 7 minutes

Nutrition Info: Calories: 206kcal, Fat: 11.3g, Carb: 3g, Proteins: 12g

Glazed Strawberry Bread

Servings: 4 Toasts

Cooking Time: 8 Minutes

Ingredients:

- 4 slices bread, ½-inch thick
- 1 cup sliced strawberries
- 1 teaspoon sugar
- Cooking spray

Directions:

1. On a clean work surface, lay the bread slices and spritz one side of each slice of bread with cooking spray.
2. Place the bread slices in the air fryer basket, sprayed side down. Top with the strawberries and a sprinkle of sugar.
3. Place the basket on the air fry position.
4. Select Air Fry, set temperature to 375ºF (190ºC), and set time to 8 minutes.
5. When cooking is complete, the toast should be well browned on each side. Remove from the air fryer grill to a plate and serve.

Fast Eggs In Bell Pepper Rings

Servings: 4

Cooking Time: 7 Minutes

Ingredients:

- 1 large yellow, red, or orange bell pepper, cut into four ¾-inch rings
- 4 eggs
- Salt and freshly ground black pepper, to taste
- 2 teaspoons salsa
- Cooking spray

Directions:

1. Coat a baking pan lightly with cooking spray.
2. Put 4 bell pepper rings in the prepared baking pan. Crack one egg into each bell pepper ring and sprinkle with salt and pepper. Top each egg with ½ teaspoon of salsa.
3. Place the pan on the bake position. Select Air Fry, set temperature to 350ºF (180ºC) and set time to 7 minutes.
4. When done, the eggs should be cooked to your desired doneness.
5. Remove the rings from the pan to a plate and serve warm.

Sausage Wraps

Servings: 2
Cooking Time: 20 Minutes

Ingredients:

- 1 cup. Mozzarella cheese
- 8 sausage
- 8 crescent rolled dough

Directions:

1. Preheat the PowerXL Air Fryer Grill by selecting bake/ pizza mode
2. Adjust temperature to 380°F and timer to 5 minutes
3. Open the dough, arrange cheese at one end of the dough
4. Add the sausage and roll, secure with a toothpick
5. Arrange the sausage wrap in the Air fryer baking tray
6. Transfer into the PowerXL Air Fryer Grill
7. Bake for 7 minutes
8. Serve and enjoy

Nutrition Info: Calories: 230kcal, Fat: 7g, Carb: 5g, Proteins: 10g

Egg Sandwich

Servings: 4
Cooking Time: 16 Minutes

Ingredients:

- 4 eggs
- 1 cup light mayonnaise
- 1 tablespoon chopped chives
- Pepper to taste
- 8 slices loaf bread

Directions:

1. Add the eggs to the air fryer rack.
2. Select air fry function.
3. Set it to 250 degrees F.
4. Cook for 16 minutes.
5. Place the eggs in a bowl with ice water.
6. Peel and transfer to another bowl.
7. Mash the eggs with a fork.
8. Stir in the mayo, chives and pepper.
9. Spread mixture on bread and top with another bread to make a sandwich.

Air Fryer Simple Grilled American Cheese Sandwich

Servings: 1 serving

Cooking Time: 10 Minutes

Ingredients:

- 2 slices Sandwich Bread
- 2-3 slices Cheddar Cheese
- 2 teaspoons Butter or Mayonnaise

Directions:

1. Place cheese between bread slices and butter the outside of both slices of bread.
2. Place in air fryer and cook at 370 degrees for 8 minutes. Flip, halfway through.
3. Crisplid Instructions
4. Place cheese between bread slices and butter the outside of both slices of bread.
5. Place tall trivet into pressure cooker and place crisplid basket on top.
6. Place sandwich into crisplid basket and place crisplid on top of pressure cooker.
7. Cook at 400 degrees for 8 minutes, flipping over after 5 minutes.

Nutrition Info: Calories: 429 Calories from Fat 252, Fat 28g, Saturated Fat 17g, Cholesterol 80mg, Sodium 664mg, Potassium 112mg, Carbohydrates 25g, Fiber 1g, Sugar 2g, Protein 18g

Engilsh Muffin Sandwiches

Servings: 4

Cooking Time: 8 Minutes

Ingredients:

- 4 English muffins, split
- 8 slices Canadian bacon
- 4 slices cheese
- Cooking spray

Directions:

1. Make the sandwiches: Top each of 4 muffin halves with 2 slices of Canadian bacon, 1 slice of cheese, and finish with the remaining muffin half.
2. Put the sandwiches in the air fryer basket and spritz the tops with cooking spray.
3. Place the basket on the bake position. Select Bake, set temperature to 370ºF (188ºC), and set time to 8 minutes.
4. When cooking is complete, remove the basket from the air fryer grill. Divide the sandwiches among four plates and serve warm.

Air Fryer Hot Dogs

Servings: 4

Cooking Time: 5 Minutes

Ingredients:

- 4 hot dogs
- 4 hot dog buns, sliced down the middle

Directions:

1. Preheat air fryer to 400 degrees.
2. Cook hot dogs for 4 minutes until cooked, moving basket once halfway through to rotate them.
3. Place hot dogs into hot dog buns.
4. Cook hot dogs in buns an additional 1-2 minutes, still at 400 degrees.
5. Enjoy immediately.
6. To air fry frozen hot dogs:
7. Preheat air fryer to 350 degrees
8. Microwave hot dogs for 30 seconds - 1 minute on defrost (optional)
9. Cook on 350 for 7-8 minutes until hot dog is heated thoroughly

Nutrition Info: Calories:: 300, Total Fat: 16g, Saturated Fat: 6g, Unsaturated Fat: 8g, Cholesterol: 28mg, Sodium: 666mg, Carbohydrates: 27g, Fiber: 1g, Sugar: 4g, Protein: 11g

Raspberry Oatmeal

Servings: 4

Cooking Time: 40 Minutes

Ingredients:

- 1 cups of shredded coconut
- 2 tsp. Stevia
- 1 tsp. Cinnamon powder
- 2 cups. Almond milk
- 1/2 cup of raspberries

Directions:

1. Mix all the ingredients in a bowl
2. Pour into the air fryer baking pan
3. Transfer to the PowerXL Air Fryer Grill
4. Using the knob, select bake/pizza mode
5. Adjust the temperature to 360°F.
6. Bake for 15 minutes
7. Serve and enjoy

Nutrition Info: Calories: 172kcal, Fat: 5g, Carb: 5g, Proteins: 6g

Scrambled Eggs

Servings: 2

Cooking Time: 5 Minutes.

Ingredients:

- 1/2 tbsp. unsalted butter
- 2 big eggs
- 1 tbsp. water kosher salt
- Fresh ground pepper

Directions:

1. Preheat the PowerXL Air Fryer Grill to 149ºC or 300ºF. Turn the fan on for air circulation.
2. Put seasoned eggs on the lightly greased pan and cover with foil.
3. Cook for 5-10 minutes or until the eggs are set
4. Use a spatula to stir the eggs, and scrape the sides.

Nutrition Info: Calories: 149kcal, Carbs: 1g, Protein: 12g, Fat: 6.7g.

Air Fryer Bacon

Servings: 6

Cooking Time: 20 Mins

Ingredients:

- ½ (16 ounce) package bacon

Directions:

1. Preheat an air fryer to 390 degrees F (200 degrees C).
2. Lay bacon in the air fryer basket in a single layer; some overlap is okay.
3. Fry for 8 minutes. Flip and continue cooking until bacon is crisp, about 7 minutes more.

Transfer cooked bacon to a plate lined with paper towels to soak up excess grease.

Nutrition Info: 67 calories; protein 4.6g 9%, carbohydrates 0.2g; fat 5.2g 8%, cholesterol 13.6mg 5%, sodium 284.9mg

Pancetta And Hotdog Omelet

Servings: 2

Cooking Time: 2o Minutes

Ingredients:

- 1 pancetta, chopped
- 1/4 tsp. dried rosemary
- 2 hot dogs, chopped
- 1/2 tsp. dried parsley
- 2 small onions, chopped

Directions:

1. In a bowl, crack the egg.
2. Add the remaining ingredients and mix, pour into the air fryer baking tray
3. Preheat the PowerXL Air Fryer Grill by selecting air fry
4. Adjust temperature to 320°F
5. Set time to 5 minutes
6. Open the door and arrange your baking pan
7. Air fry for 10 minutes
8. Serve and enjoy

Nutrition Info: Calories: 185kcal, Fat: 10.5g, Carb: 6g, Proteins: 15g

Fast Breakfast Sandwiches

Servings: 2

Cooking Time: 8 Minutes

Ingredients:

- 1 teaspoon butter, softened
- 4 slices bread
- 4 slices smoked country ham
- 4 slices Cheddar cheese
- 4 thick slices tomato

Directions:

1. Spoon ½ teaspoon of butter onto one side of 2 slices of bread and spread it all over.
2. Assemble the sandwiches: Top each of 2 slices of unbuttered bread with 2 slices of ham, 2 slices of cheese, and 2 slices of tomato. Place the remaining 2 slices of bread on top, butter-side up.
3. Lay the sandwiches in the air fryer basket, buttered side down.
4. Place the basket on the bake position. Select Bake, set temperature to 370ºF (188ºC), and set time to 8 minutes. Flip the sandwiches halfway through the cooking time.
5. When cooking is complete, the sandwiches should be golden brown on both sides and the cheese should be melted. Remove from the air fryer grill. Allow to cool for 5 minutes before slicing to serve.

Breakfast Egg And Tomatoes

Servings: 2

Cooking Time: 30 Minutes

Ingredients:

- Salt and pepper to taste
- 2 eggs
- 2 large tomatoes

Directions:

1. Preheat the air fryer by selecting the bake/pizza mode.
2. Adjust the temperature to 375°F
3. Cut off the top of the tomatoes, scoop out the seed and flesh.
4. Break the egg into each tomato, transfer to the PowerXL air fryer baking tray.
5. Bake for 24 minutes
6. Serve and enjoy

Nutrition Info: Calories: 95kcal, Fat: 5g, Carb: 5.5g, Proteins: 7g

Baked Eggs In Avocado

Servings: 2
Cooking Time: 9 Minutes

Ingredients:

- 1 large avocado, halved and pitted
- 2 large eggs
- 2 tomato slices, divided
- ½ cup nonfat Cottage cheese, divided
- ½ teaspoon fresh cilantro, for garnish

Directions:

1. Line the sheet pan with the aluminium foil.
2. Slice a thin piece from the bottom of each avocado half so they sit flat. Remove a small amount from each avocado half to make a bigger hole to hold the egg.
3. Arrange the avocado halves on the pan, hollow-side up. Break 1 egg into each half. Top each half with 1 tomato slice and ¼ cup of the Cottage cheese.
4. Place the pan on the bake position.
5. Select Bake, set temperature to 425ºF (220ºC) and set time to 9 minutes.
6. When cooking is complete, remove the pan from the air fryer grill. Garnish with the fresh cilantro and serve.

Bacon Knots

Servings: 6

Cooking Time: 7 To 8 Minutes

Ingredients:

- 1 pound (454 g) maple smoked center-cut bacon
- ¼ cup brown sugar
- ¼ cup maple syrup
- Coarsely cracked black peppercorns, to taste

Directions:

1. On a clean work surface, tie each bacon strip in a loose knot.
2. Stir together the brown sugar and maple syrup in a bowl. Generously brush this mixture over the bacon knots.
3. Place the bacon knots in the air fryer basket and sprinkle with the coarsely cracked black peppercorns.
4. Place the basket on the bake position. Select Air Fry, set temperature to 390ºF (199ºC), and set time to 8 minutes.
5. After 5 minutes, remove the basket from the air fryer grill and flip the bacon knots. Return the basket to the air fryer grill and continue cooking for 2 to 3 minutes more.
6. When cooking is complete, the bacon should be crisp. Remove from the air fryer grill to a paper towel-lined plate. Let the bacon knots cool for a few minutes and serve warm.

French Toast

Servings: 4

Cooking Time: 10 Minutes

Ingredients:

- 2 slices of bread
- 1 tsp. Liquid vanilla
- 3 eggs
- 1 tbsp. Margarine

Directions:

1. Preheat the PowerXL Air Fryer Grill by setting it to toast/pizza mode.
2. Adjust the temperature to 375°F; insert the pizza tray.
3. In a bowl, whisk the eggs and vanilla
4. Spread the margarine on the bread, transfer into the egg and allow to soak
5. Place on the PowerXL air fryer pizza rack and set time to 6 minutes, flip after 3 minutes.

Nutrition Info: Calories: 99kcal, Fat: 0.2g, Carb: 7g, Proteins: 5g

FISH AND SEAFOOD RECIPES

Golden Fish Sticks

Servings: 8
Cooking Time: 6 Minutes

Ingredients:

- 8 ounces (227 g) fish fillets (pollock or cod), cut into ½ × 3 inches strips
- Salt, to taste (optional)
- ½ cup plain bread crumbs
- Cooking spray

Directions:

1. Season the fish strips with salt to taste, if desired.
2. Place the bread crumbs on a plate, then roll the fish in the bread crumbs until well coated. Spray all sides of the fish with cooking spray. Transfer to the air fry basket in a single layer.
3. Place the basket on the air fry position.
4. Select Air Fry, set temperature to 400ºF (205ºC), and set time to 6 minutes.
5. When cooked, the fish sticks should be golden brown and crispy. Remove from the air fryer grill to a plate and serve hot.

Shrimp Bang Bang

Servings: 4
Cooking Time: 4 Minutes

Ingredients:

- 1 cup cornstarch
- ¼ teaspoon Sriracha powder
- 2 lb. shrimp, peeled and deveined
- ¼ cup mayonnaise
- ¼ cup sweet chili sauce

Directions:

1. In a bowl, combine cornstarch and Sriracha powder.
2. Dredge shrimp with this mixture.
3. Place shrimp in the air fryer.
4. Choose air fry setting.
5. Cook at 400 degrees F for 7 minutes per side.
6. Mix the mayo and chili sauce.
7. Serve shrimp with sauce.

Grilled Mustard Salmon

Servings: 2

Cooking Time: 25 Minutes

Ingredients:

- 1 tbsp of coconut oil
- 2 large salmon fillets
- 2 tbsp of mustard
- 1 tbsp of maple extract
- Black pepper and salt

Directions:

1. Mix mustard, salmon, maple extract, pepper, and salt in a bowl.
2. Drizzle the fish with cooking oil.
3. Place the fish on the PowerXL Air Fryer Grill basket at position 6.
4. Set the PowerXL Air Fryer Grill to Air fryer/Grill.
5. Set the timer to 10 minutes at 370ºF.
6. Serve immediately.

Nutrition Info: Calories: 300kcal, Fat: 22g, Carb: 2.5g, Proteins: 25g

Healthy Air Fryer Baked Salmon

Servings: 2

Cooking Time: 13 Mins

Ingredients:

- 2 6 ounce salmon fillets , skin and bones removed
- 1 teaspoon olive oil or light spray of organic cooking spray
- kosher salt , to taste
- black pepper , to taste

Directions:

1. Coat salmon with lightly oil or cooking spray. Season both sides of salmon with salt and pepper.
2. Place salmon in basket. Air fry the salmon at 360°F for about 10 minutes or until cooked to your preferred texture.
3. Check the salmon with a fork to make sure it's cooked the way you like it.
4. Enjoy! It's that easy.

Nutrition Info: Calories: 259 Calories from Fat 108, Fat 12g, Saturated Fat 1g, Cholesterol 93mg, Sodium 74mg, Potassium 833mg, Protein 33g

Air Fryer Mahi Mahi With Brown Butter

Servings: 4
Cooking Time: 20 Mins

Ingredients:

- 4 (6 ounce) mahi mahi fillets
- salt and ground black pepper to taste
- cooking spray
- ⅔ cup butter

Directions:

1. Preheat an air fryer to 350 degrees F (175 degrees C).
2. Season mahi mahi fillets with salt and pepper and spray with cooking spray on both sides. Place fillets in the air fryer basket, making sure to leave space in between.
3. Cook until fish flakes easily with a fork and has a golden hue, about 12 minutes.
4. While fish is cooking, melt butter in a small saucepan over medium-low heat. Bring butter to a simmer and cook until butter turns frothy and a rich brown color, 3 to 5 minutes. Remove from heat.
5. Transfer fish fillets to a plate and drizzle with brown butter.

Nutrition Info: 416 calories; protein 31.8g; carbohydratesg; fat 31.9g; cholesterol 205.4mg; sodium 406.3mg

Fast Bacon-wrapped Scallops

Servings: 4
Cooking Time: 10 Minutes

Ingredients:

- 8 slices bacon, cut in half
- 16 sea scallops, patted dry
- Cooking spray
- Salt and freshly ground black pepper, to taste
- 16 toothpicks, soaked in water for at least 30 minutes

Directions:

1. On a clean work surface, wrap half of a slice of bacon around each scallop and secure with a toothpick.
2. Lay the bacon-wrapped scallops in the air fry basket in a single layer.
3. Spritz the scallops with cooking spray and sprinkle the salt and pepper to season.
4. Place the basket on the air fry position.
5. Select Air Fry, set temperature to 370ºF (188ºC), and set time to 10 minutes. Flip the scallops halfway through the cooking time.
6. When cooking is complete, the bacon should be cooked through and the scallops should be firm. Remove the scallops from the air fryer grill to a plate Serve warm.

Lemony Tilapia Fillet

Servings: 4
Cooking Time: 12 Minutes

Ingredients:

- 1 tablespoon olive oil
- 1 tablespoon lemon juice
- 1 teaspoon minced garlic
- ½ teaspoon chili powder
- 4 tilapia fillets

Directions:

1. Line a baking pan with parchment paper.
2. In a shallow bowl, stir together the lemon juice, olive oil, chili powder, and garlic to make a marinade. Put the tilapia fillets in the bowl, turning to coat evenly.
3. Place the fillets in the baking pan in a single layer.
4. Slide the pan into the air fryer grill.
5. Select Air Fry, set temperature to 375ºF (190ºC), and set time to 12 minutes.
6. When cooked, the fish will flake apart with a fork. Remove from the air fryer grill to a plate and serve hot.

Simple Air-fried Scallops

Servings: 2

Cooking Time: 4 Minutes

Ingredients:

- 12 medium sea scallops, rinsed and patted dry
- 1 teaspoon fine sea salt
- ¾ teaspoon ground black pepper, plus more for garnish
- Fresh thyme leaves, for garnish (optional)
- Avocado oil spray

Directions:

1. Coat the air fry basket with avocado oil spray.
2. Place the scallops in a medium bowl and spritz with avocado oil spray. Sprinkle the salt and pepper to season.
3. Transfer the seasoned scallops to the air fry basket, spacing them apart.
4. Place the basket on the air fry position.
5. Select Air Fry, set temperature to 390ºF (199ºC), and set time to 4 minutes. Flip the scallops halfway through the cooking time.
6. When cooking is complete, the scallops should reach an internal temperature of just 145ºF (63ºC) on a meat thermometer. Remove the basket from the air fryer grill. Sprinkle the pepper and thyme leaves on top for garnish, if desired. Serve immediately.

Pesto Salmon

Servings: 4

Cooking Time: 35 Minutes

Ingredients:

- 4 salmon fillets, 1-1/4 lb. each
- 2 tbsp. thawed pesto
- 2 tbsp. white wine vinegar
- 1 lemon, cut into halves
- 2 tbsp. Toasted pine nuts

Directions:

1. Place the salmon fillets on the pan after spraying cooking spray
2. Preheat the PowerXL Air Fryer Grill to 232ºC or 450ºF.
3. Marinade the fillets with lemon juice, pesto, and white wine vinegar
4. Broil for 15 minutes.

Nutrition Info: Calories: 326kcal, Carbs: 1.5g, Protein: 39g, Fat: 17g.

Swordfish Steak In The Air Fryer

Servings: 2

Cooking Time: 40 Mins

Ingredients:

- swordfish steak
- seasoning of your choice, cooking oil spray

Directions:

1. Use the cooking spray to add a bit of oil to the swordfish.
2. Rub your choice of seasonings onto the swordfish, letting it marinate for at least 20 minutes.
3. Preheat the airfryer to 204ºC or 400ºF.
4. Spray the airfryer basket with cooking spray to avoid the swordfish from sticking.
5. Cook the swordfish for 8-10 minutes, flipping halfway through to assure even cooking.

Nutrition Info: Calories 310, Fat 7g, Saturated Fat 3g, Potassium 762mg, Sugar 3g, Protein 29g

Garlic Butter Orange Roughy

Servings: 4

Cooking Time: 30 Minutes

Ingredients:

- 2 tbsp. butter
- 1/2 lb. orange Roughy, filleted
- 1 tbsp. olive oil
- 3 minced garlic cloves
- Salt & pepper

Directions:

1. Preheat the PowerXL Air Fryer Grill to 190ºC or 375ºF.
2. Melt butter in a pan with garlic cloves and olive oil.
3. Season the fillets and pour the garlic butter.
4. Bake for 20 minutes

Nutrition Info: Calories: 255kcal, Carbs: 2g, Protein: 19g, Fat: 19g.

Panko-crusted Fish Sticks

Servings: 8 Fish Sticks

Cooking Time: 8 Minutes

Ingredients:

- 8 ounces (227 g) fish fillets (pollock or cod), cut into ½×3-inch strips
- Salt, to taste (optional)
- ½ cup plain bread crumbs
- Cooking spray

Directions:

1. Season the fish strips with salt to taste, if desired.
2. Place the bread crumbs on a plate. Roll the fish strips in the bread crumbs to coat. Spritz the fish strips with cooking spray.
3. Arrange the fish strips in the air fry basket in a single layer.
4. Place the basket on the air fry position.
5. Air Fry, set temperature to 390ºF (199ºC), and set time to 8 minutes.
6. When cooking is complete, they should be golden brown. Remove from the air fryer grill and cool for 5 minutes before serving.

MEAT RECIPES

Air Fryer Beef Steak

Servings: 4
Cooking Time: 20 Minutes

Ingredients:

- 2 lb. Ribeye steak
- Salt and pepper to taste
- 1 tbsp. Olive oil

Directions:

1. Preheat the PowerXL Air Fryer Grill by selecting air fry mode
2. Adjust temperature to 356°F and timer to 5 minutes
3. Season the steak with olive oil, salt, and pepper.
4. Place on the Air fryer pizza tray
5. Transfer into the PowerXL Air Fryer Grill
6. Air fry for 7 minutes, flip and cook for additional 6 minutes
7. Serve and enjoy

Nutrition Info: Calories: 230kcal, Fat: 17g, Carb: 1g, Proteins: 23g

Beef And Potatoes

Servings: 2
Cooking Time: 15 Minutes

Ingredients:

- 1 lb. Ground beef
- 3 cups of mashed potatoes
- 1 cup sour cream
- 2 eggs
- 2 tbsp. Garlic powder

Directions:

1. Preheat the PowerXL Air Fryer Grill by selecting bake/pizza mode
2. Adjust temperature to 350°F and time to 5 minutes
3. Combine all the ingredients in a bowl.
4. Pour into the Air fryer baking tray
5. Transfer into the PowerXL Air Fryer Grill
6. Bake for 6 minutes
7. Serve and enjoy!

Nutrition Info: Calories: 320kcal, Fat: 7g, Carb: 9g, Proteins: 27g

Roasted Lamb

Servings: 4

Cooking Time: 1hour 13 Minutes

Ingredients:

- 2-1/2 pounds lamb leg roast, slits carved
- 1 tbsp olive oil
- 2 garlic cloves, sliced into smaller slithers
- 1 tbsp dried rosemary
- Cracked Himalayan rock salt and cracked peppercorns, to taste

Directions:

1. Make the cuts in the lamb roast and insert them with garlic.
2. Sprinkle the lamb roast with kosher salt, rosemary, and ground black pepper.
3. Brush with oil.
4. Preheat the PowerXL Air Fryer Grill by selecting air fry mode.
5. Adjust the temperature to 380°F, set time to 5 minutes
6. Place the lamb roast on the Baking Pan
7. Transfer to the PowerXL Air Fryer Grill.
8. Air fry for 1 hour 15 minutes
9. Serve and enjoy

Nutrition Info: Calories: 246kcal, Fat: 7g, Carb: 9g, Proteins: 33g

Panko-crusted Pork Cutlet

Servings: 4

Cooking Time: 10 Minutes

Ingredients:

- $^{2}/_{3}$ cup all-purpose flour
- 2 large egg whites
- 1 cup panko bread crumbs
- 4 (4-ounce / 113-g) center-cut boneless pork loin chops (about ½ inch thick)
- Cooking spray

Directions:

1. Pour the flour in a bowl. Whisk the egg whites in a separate bowl. Spread the bread crumbs on a large plate.
2. Dredge the pork loin chops in the flour first, press to coat well, then shake the excess off and dunk the chops in the eggs whites, and then roll the chops over the bread crumbs. Shake the excess off.
3. Arrange the pork chops in the air fry basket and spritz with cooking spray.
4. Place the basket on the air fry position.
5. Select Air Fry. Set temperature to 375ºF (190ºC) and set time to 10 minutes.
6. After 5 minutes, remove the basket from the air fryer grill. Flip the pork chops. Return the basket to the air fryer grill and continue cooking.
7. When cooking is complete, the pork chops should be crunchy and lightly browned.
8. Serve immediately.

Barbecue Pork Tenderloin

Servings: 2

Cooking Time: 20 Minutes

Ingredients:

- ½ lb. pork tenderloin, diced
- ¼ cup barbecue sauce
- 1 teaspoon olive oil

Directions:

1. Coat the pork tenderloin in olive oil.
2. Brush with barbecue sauce.
3. Place in the air fryer rack.
4. Choose grill function.
5. Cook at 375 degrees F for 15 to 20 minutes.

Pork Chop With Worcestershire Sauce

Servings: 2

Cooking Time: 20 Minutes

Ingredients:

- 2 (10-ounce / 284-g) bone-in, center cut pork chops, 1-inch thick
- 2 teaspoons Worcestershire sauce
- Salt and ground black pepper, to taste
- Cooking spray

Directions:

1. Rub the Worcestershire sauce on both sides of pork chops.
2. Season with salt and pepper.
3. Spritz the air fry basket with cooking spray and place the chops in the air fry basket side by side.
4. Place the basket on the toast position.
5. Select Toast. Set the temperature to 350ºF (180ºC) and set the time to 20 minutes.
6. After 10 minutes, remove the basket from the air fryer grill. Flip the pork chops with tongs. Return the basket to the air fryer grill and continue cooking.
7. When cooking is complete, the pork should be well browned on both sides.
8. Let rest for 5 minutes before serving.

Perfect Rump Roast

Servings: 5

Cooking Time: 2 Hours

Ingredients:

- 4lb rump roast
- 3 Garlic cloves
- 1 tbsp. each of salt, pepper
- 1 onion
- 1 cup water

Directions:

1. Preheat the PowerXL Air Fryer Grill to 260ºC or 500ºF
2. Make 4-5 cuts on the roast, and fill with salt, pepper, and garlic.
3. Season some more before searing for 20 mins. Add water and minced onion.
4. Cook in the PowerXL Air Fryer Grill at 180ºC or 350ºF for 1.5 hours.

Nutrition Info: Calories: 916.8kcal, Carbs: 4.4g, Protein: 94.6g, Fat: 55.2g.

Ribeye Steaks With Worcestershire Sauce

Servings: 2 To 4

Cooking Time: 10 To 12 Minutes

Ingredients:

- 2 (8-ounce / 227-g) boneless ribeye steaks
- 4 teaspoons Worcestershire sauce
- ½ teaspoon garlic powder
- Salt and ground black pepper, to taste
- 4 teaspoons olive oil

Directions:

1. Brush the steaks with Worcestershire sauce on both sides. Sprinkle with coarsely ground black pepper and garlic powder. Drizzle the steaks with olive oil. Allow steaks to marinate for 30 minutes.
2. Transfer the steaks in the air fry basket.
3. Place the basket on the toast position.
4. Select Toast. Set the temperature to 400ºF (205ºC) and set time to 4 minutes.
5. After 2 minutes, remove the basket from the air fryer grill. Flip the steaks. Return the basket to the air fryer grill and continue cooking.
6. When cooking is complete, the steaks should be well browned.
7. Remove the steaks from the air fry basket and let sit for 5 minutes. Salt and serve.

Pork Belly Bites

Servings: 4

Cooking Time: 20 Minutes

Ingredients:

- 1 lb. pork belly, diced
- Salt and pepper to taste
- ½ teaspoon garlic powder
- 1 teaspoon Worcestershire sauce

Directions:

1. Select the grill setting in your air fryer.
2. Preheat it to 400 degrees F.
3. Season pork with salt, pepper, garlic powder and Worcestershire sauce.
4. Add to the air fryer.
5. Cook at 400 degrees F for 20 minutes, flipping twice.

Sirloin Roast Beef

Servings: 6

Cooking Time: 1 Hour 45 Minutes

Ingredients:

- 3.3 lbs. Sirloin of Beef
- 2 tbsp. vegetable oil
- 6 ounces red wine
- 14 ounces beef consomme

Directions:

1. Preheat the PowerXL Air Fryer Grill to 200ºC or 400ºF.
2. Season the sirloin and cook it at medium heat in oil for 5 mins, turning regularly.
3. Roast it in the PowerXL Air Fryer Grill for 15 mins to make it medium-rare. Flip it halfway.
4. Remove it when the internal temperature is 145ºF, and cover with foil.
5. Make a gravy with the fat residue on the pan and some wine.
6. Add beef consomme to the sauce and simmer for 5 mins. Strain when completed and pour on the roast.

Nutrition Info: Calories: 179kcal, Protein: 22g, Fat: 9.4g.

Salt-and-pepper Beef Roast

Servings: 12-14

Cooking Time: 4.5 Hours

Ingredients:

- 4-6lbs boned beef cross rib roast
- 1/4 cup coarse salt
- 1/4 cup sugar
- 2 tbsp. coarse-ground pepper
- 1/2 cup prepared horseradish

Directions:

1. Mix salt with sugar in a bowl. Pat the mixture on the beef, and marinate for 3-4 hours.
2. Mix 1.5 tsp. salt, pepper, and horseradish.
3. Put the beef on a rack in a 9"x13" pan and rub the horseradish mixture.
4. Roast in 176ºC or 350ºF in the PowerXL Air Fryer Grill. Check if the internal temperature is 120-125ºC.
5. Rest for 20 minutes, and then slice the meat thinly across the grain.

Nutrition Info: Calories: 267kcal, Carbs: 1.3g, Protein: 20g, Fat: 19g.

Bbq Lamb

Servings: 8

Cooking Time: 1hour 40 Minutes

Ingredients:

- 4 lbs boneless leg of lamb, cut into 2-inch chunks
- 2-1/2 tbsps herb salt
- 2 tbsps olive oil

Directions:

1. Preheat the PowerXL Air Fryer Grill by selecting air fryer mode
2. Adjust the temperature to 390°F, set time to 5 minutes
3. Season the meat with salt and olive oil
4. Arrange on the Air fryer baking tray
5. Transfer to the PowerXL Air Fryer Grill
6. Air fry for 15 minutes, flipping halfway through
7. Serve and enjoy

Nutrition Info: Calories: 341kcal, Fat: 16g, Carb: 1g, Proteins: 26g

Beef Tenderloin

Servings: 6

Cooking Time: 1 Hour 10 Minutes

Ingredients:

- 5 lbs. Beef Tenderloin
- Vegetable Oil
- Spices, salt, and pepper

Directions:

1. Preheat the PowerXL Air Fryer Grill to 180ºC or 350ºF. Cut extra fat from it.
2. Gently rub tenderloin with vegetable oil and seasoning.
3. Cook it in the PowerXL Air Fryer Grill for 20-30 mins.

Nutrition Info: Calories: 179kcal, Protein: 26g, Fat: 7.6g.

Pan-seared Roasted Strip Steak

Servings: 2

Cooking Time: 30 Minutes

Ingredients:

- One 3-inch Strip Steak
- 1 tbsp. Butter
- Meat Tenderizer
- Coarsely Ground Black Pepper

Directions:

1. Cut and season the room-temperature meat.
2. Preheat the PowerXL Air Fryer Grill to 200ºC or 400ºF.
3. Sear steak in butter over medium-high heat evenly for 2-3 mins after an hour of resting.
4. Cook in the PowerXL Air Fryer Grill for 7 mins to achieve medium-rare.

Nutrition Info: Calories: 253.6kcal, Carbs: 0.2g, Protein: 21.1g, Fat: 18.1g, .

Bacon & Broccoli Rice Bowl

Servings: 4

Cooking Time: 10 Minutes

Ingredients:

- 8 slices bacon
- 4 cups cooked rice
- 4 cups broccoli, steamed
- 1 carrot, sliced into thin sticks

Directions:

1. Add the bacon to the air fryer.
2. Set it to air fry.
3. Cook at 400 degrees F for 10 minutes or until crispy.
4. Add rice to serving bowls.
5. Top with the bacon, broccoli and carrots.

Prime Rib Roast

Servings: 4-6

Cooking Time: 1 Hr 45 Mins

Ingredients:

- Prime Rib Roast
- Butter
- Salt and pepper

Directions:

1. Cut the fat parts from each side of the meat, and put it inside the PowerXL Air Fryer Grill.
2. Cook at 230ºC or 450ºF for 15 minutes. Lower it to 165ºC or 325 afterward.
3. Check if the internal temperature has reached 110ºC or 225ºF and serve.

Nutrition Info: Calories: 290kcal, Protein: 19.2g, Fat: 23.1g.

Golden Pork Tenderloin

Servings: 6

Cooking Time: 10 Minutes

Ingredients:

- 2 large egg whites
- 1½ tablespoons Dijon mustard
- 2 cups crushed pretzel crumbs
- 1½ pounds (680 g) pork tenderloin, cut into ¼-pound (113-g) sections
- Cooking spray

Directions:

1. Spritz the air fry basket with cooking spray.
2. Whisk the egg whites with Dijon mustard in a bowl until bubbly. Pour the pretzel crumbs in a separate bowl.
3. Dredge the pork tenderloin in the egg white mixture and press to coat. Shake the excess off and roll the tenderloin over the pretzel crumbs.
4. Arrange the well-coated pork tenderloin in the basket and spritz with cooking spray.
5. Place the basket on the air fry position.
6. Select Air Fry. Set temperature to 350ºF (180ºC) and set time to 10 minutes.
7. After 5 minutes, remove the basket from the air fryer grill. Flip the pork. Return the basket to the air fryer grill and continue cooking.
8. When cooking is complete, the pork should be golden brown and crispy.
9. Serve immediately.

Breaded Beef Schnitzel

Servings: 2

Cooking Time: 20 Minutes

Ingredients:

- 4 beef schnitzel
- 2 tbsp. Olive oil
- 1 egg
- 5 cup of breadcrumbs

Directions:

1. Preheat the PowerXL Air Fryer Grill by selecting grill mode
2. Adjust temperature to 350°F and time to 5 minutes
3. Whisk egg and olive oil in a bowl
4. Add breadcrumbs to another bowl
5. Dip the beef schnitzel in the egg mixture.
6. then coat with the breadcrumb mixture
7. Arrange on the grilling plate
8. Transfer into the PowerXL Air Fryer Grill
9. Grill for 12 minutes, flipping halfway
10. Serve and enjoy!

Nutrition Info: Calories: 256kcal, Fat: 5g, Carb: 12g, Proteins: 15g

VEGAN AND VEGETARIAN RECIPES

Easy Maple And Pecan Granola

Servings: 4
Cooking Time: 20 Minutes

Ingredients:

- 1½ cups rolled oats
- ¼ cup maple syrup
- ¼ cup pecan pieces
- 1 teaspoon vanilla extract
- ½ teaspoon ground cinnamon

Directions:

1. Line a baking sheet with parchment paper.
2. Mix together the oats, pecan pieces, maple syrup, cinnamon, and vanilla in a large bowl and stir until the oats and pecan pieces are completely coated. Spread the mixture evenly on the baking sheet.
3. Place the baking sheet on the bake position.
4. Select Bake, set temperature to 300ºF (150ºC), and set time to 20 minutes. Stir once halfway through the cooking time.
5. When done, remove from the air fryer grill and cool for 30 minutes before serving. The granola may still be a bit soft right after removing, but it will gradually firm up as it cools.

Honey Toasted Carrots

Servings: 4
Cooking Time: 12 Minutes
Ingredients:

- 1 pound (454 g) baby carrots
- 2 tablespoons olive oil
- 1 tablespoon honey
- 1 teaspoon dried dill
- Salt and black pepper, to taste

Directions:

1. Place the carrots in a large bowl. Add the honey, olive oil, salt, dill, and pepper and toss to coat well.
2. Transfer the carrots to the air fry basket.
3. Place the basket on the toast position.
4. Select Toast, set temperature to 350ºF (180ºC), and set time to 12 minutes. Stir the carrots once during cooking.
5. When cooking is complete, the carrots should be crisp-tender. Remove from the air fryer grill and serve warm.

Cheesy Egg Rolls

Servings: 12
Cooking Time: 12 Minutes
Ingredients:

- 12 spring roll wrappers
- 12 slices provolone cheese
- 3 eggs, cooked and sliced
- 1 carrot, sliced into thin strips
- 1 tablespoon water

Directions:

1. Top the wrappers with cheese, eggs and carrot strips.
2. Roll up the wrappers and seal with water.
3. Place inside the air fryer.
4. Set it to air fry.
5. Cook at 390 degrees F for 12 minutes, turning once or twice.

Brussels Sprout With Tomatoes Mix

Servings: 3

Cooking Time: 20 Minutes

Ingredients:

- 6 halved cherry tomatoes
- 1 tbsp of olive oil
- 1 pound of Brussel sprouts
- Black pepper and salt
- 1/4 cup of chopped green onions

Directions:

1. Sprinkle pepper and salt on the Brussels sprout.
2. Place it on the PowerXL Air Fryer Grill pan.
3. Set the PowerXL Air Fryer Grill to air fry function.
4. Cook for 10 minutes at 350ºF.
5. Place the cooked sprout in a bowl, add pepper, green onion, salt, olive oil, and cherry tomatoes.
6. Mix well and serve immediately

Nutrition Info: Calories: 57kcal, Fat: 1g, Carb: 12g, Proteins: 5g

Green Beans With Sesame Seeds

Servings: 4
Cooking Time: 8 Minutes

Ingredients:

- 1 tablespoon reduced-sodium soy sauce or tamari
- ½ tablespoon Sriracha sauce
- 4 teaspoons toasted sesame oil, divided
- 12 ounces (340 g) trimmed green beans
- ½ tablespoon toasted sesame seeds

Directions:

1. Whisk together the Sriracha sauce, soy sauce, and 1 teaspoon of sesame oil in a small bowl until smooth. Set aside.
2. Toss the green beans with the remaining sesame oil in a large bowl until evenly coated.
3. Place the green beans in the air fry basket in a single layer.
4. Place the basket on the air fry position.
5. Select Air Fry, set temperature to 375ºF (190ºC), and set time to 8 minutes. Stir the green beans halfway through the cooking time.
6. When cooking is complete, the green beans should be lightly charred and tender. Remove from the air fryer grill to a platter. Pour the prepared sauce over the top of green beans and toss well. Serve sprinkled with the toasted sesame seeds.

Butter Toasted Cremini Mushrooms

Servings: about 1½ Cups

Cooking Time: 30 Minutes

Ingredients:

- 1 pound (454 g) button or cremini mushrooms, washed, stems trimmed, and cut into quarters or thick slices
- ¼ cup water
- 1 teaspoon kosher salt or ½ teaspoon fine salt
- 3 tablespoons unsalted butter, cut into pieces, or extra-virgin olive oil

Directions:

1. Place a large piece of aluminum foil on the sheet pan. Place the mushroom pieces in the middle of the foil. Spread them out into an even layer. Pour the water over them, season with the salt, and add the butter. Wrap the mushrooms in the foil.
2. Place the pan on the toast position.
3. Select Toast, set the temperature to 325ºF (163ºC), and set the time for 15 minutes.
4. After 15 minutes, remove the pan from the air fryer grill. Transfer the foil packet to a cutting board and carefully unwrap it. Pour the mushrooms and cooking liquid from the foil onto the sheet pan.
5. Place the basket on the toast position.
6. Select Toast, set the temperature to 350ºF (180ºC), and set the time for 15 minutes.
7. After about 10 minutes, remove the pan from the air fryer grill and stir the mushrooms. Return the pan to the air fryer grill and continue cooking for anywhere from 5 to 15 more minutes, or until the liquid is mostly gone and the mushrooms start to brown.
8. Serve immediately.

Brussels Sprout Chips

Servings: 2

Cooking Time: 15 Minutes

Ingredients:

- 2 cups Brussels sprouts, sliced thinly
- 1 tablespoon olive oil
- 1 teaspoon garlic powder
- Salt and pepper to taste
- 2 tablespoons Parmesan cheese, grated

Directions:

1. Toss the Brussels sprouts in oil.
2. Sprinkle with garlic powder, salt, pepper and Parmesan cheese.
3. Choose bake function.
4. Add the Brussels sprouts in the air fryer.
5. Cook at 350 degrees F for 8 minutes.
6. Flip and cook for 7 more minutes.

Cheesy Brussels Sprouts

Servings: 4

Cooking Time: 20 Minutes

Ingredients:

- 1 pound (454 g) fresh Brussels sprouts, trimmed
- 1 tablespoon olive oil
- ½ teaspoon salt
- ⅛ teaspoon pepper
- ¼ cup grated Parmesan cheese

Directions:

1. In a large bowl, combine the Brussels sprouts with salt, olive oil, and pepper and toss until evenly coated.
2. Spread the Brussels sprouts evenly in the air fry basket.
3. Place the air fry basket on the air fry position.
4. Select Air Fry, set temperature to 330ºF (166ºC), and set time to 20 minutes. Stir the Brussels sprouts twice during cooking.
5. When cooking is complete, the Brussels sprouts should be golden brown and crisp. Remove the basket from the air fryer grill. Sprinkle the grated Parmesan cheese on top and serve warm.

Broccoli Salad

Servings: 4
Cooking Time: 20 Minutes

Ingredients:

- 6 cloves of garlic
- 1 head of broccoli
- Black pepper and salt
- 1 tbsp of Chinese rice wine vinegar
- 1 tbsp of peanut oil

Directions:

1. Mix oil, salt, broccoli, and pepper.
2. Place the mixture on the PowerXL Air Fryer Grill pan.
3. Set the PowerXL Air Fryer Grill to air fry function.
4. Cook for 9 minutes at 350ºF.
5. Place the broccoli in the salad bowl and add peanuts oil, rice vinegar, and garlic.
6. Serve immediately.

Nutrition Info: Calories: 199kcal, Fat: 14g, Carb: 17g, Proteins: 8g

Zucchini Lasagna

Servings: 4
Cooking Time: 15 Minutes

Ingredients:

- 1 zucchini, sliced thinly lengthwise and divided
- ½ cup marinara sauce, divided
- ¼ cup ricotta, divided
- 1 cup fresh basil leaves, chopped and divided
- ¼ cup spinach leaves, chopped and divided

Directions:

1. Layer half of the zucchini slices in a small loaf pan.
2. Spread with half of marinara sauce and ricotta.
3. Top with half of spinach and basil.
4. Repeat layers with the remaining ingredients.
5. Cover the pan with foil.
6. Place inside the air fryer.
7. Set it to bake.
8. Cook at 400 degrees F for 10 minutes.
9. Remove foil and cook for another 5 minutes.

Cheesy Brussels Sprout

Servings: 3

Cooking Time: 20 Minutes

Ingredients:

- 1 lemon juice
- 2 tbsp of butter
- 1 pound of Brussel sprout
- 3 tbsp of grated parmesan
- Black pepper and salt

Directions:

1. Place the Brussel sprout on the PowerXL Air Fryer Grill pan.
2. Set the PowerXL Air Fryer Grill to air fry function.
3. Cook for 8 minutes at 350ºF.
4. Heat butter in a pan over medium heat, add pepper, lemon juice, and salt.
5. Add Brussel sprout and parmesan.
6. Serve immediately.

Nutrition Info: Calories: 75kcal, Fat: 5g, Carb: 8g, Proteins: 6g

Smoked Paprika Cauliflower Florets

Servings: 4

Cooking Time: 20 Minutes

Ingredients:

- 1 large head cauliflower, broken into small florets
- 2 teaspoons smoked paprika
- 1 teaspoon garlic powder
- Salt and freshly ground black pepper, to taste
- Cooking spray

Directions:

1. Spray the air fry basket with cooking spray.
2. In a medium bowl, toss the cauliflower florets with the smoked paprika and garlic powder until evenly coated. Sprinkle with salt and pepper.
3. Place the cauliflower florets in the air fry basket and lightly mist with cooking spray.
4. Place the air fry basket on the air fry position.
5. Select Air Fry, set temperature to 400ºF (205ºC), and set time to 20 minutes. Stir the cauliflower four times during cooking.
6. Remove the cauliflower from the air fryer grill and serve hot.

Crispy Zucchini Rounds

Servings: 4

Cooking Time: 14 Minutes

Ingredients:

- 2 zucchini, sliced into ¼- to ½-inch-thick rounds (about 2 cups)
- ¼ teaspoon garlic granules
- ⅛ teaspoon sea salt
- Freshly ground black pepper, to taste (optional)
- Cooking spray

Directions:

1. Spritz the air fry basket with cooking spray.
2. Put the zucchini rounds in the air fry basket, spreading them out as much as possible. Top with a sprinkle of sea salt, garlic granules, and black pepper (if desired). Spritz the zucchini rounds with cooking spray.
3. Place the basket on the toast position.
4. Select Toast, set temperature to 392ºF (200ºC), and set time to 14 minutes. Flip the zucchini rounds halfway through.
5. When cooking is complete, the zucchini rounds should be crisp-tender. Remove from the air fryer grill. Let them rest for 5 minutes and serve.

Balsamic Asparagus Spears

Servings: 4

Cooking Time: 10 Minutes

Ingredients:

- 4 tablespoons olive oil, plus more for greasing
- 4 tablespoons balsamic vinegar
- 1½ pounds (680 g) asparagus spears, trimmed
- Salt and freshly ground black pepper, to taste

Directions:

1. Grease the air fry basket with olive oil.
2. In a shallow bowl, stir together the 4 tablespoons of olive oil and balsamic vinegar to make a marinade.
3. Put the asparagus spears in the bowl so they are thoroughly covered by the marinade and allow to marinate for 5 minutes.
4. Put the asparagus in the greased basket in a single layer and season with salt and pepper.
5. Place the air fry basket on the air fry position.
6. Select Air Fry, set temperature to 350ºF (180ºC), and set time to 10 minutes. Flip the asparagus halfway through the cooking time.
7. When done, the asparagus should be tender and lightly browned. Cool for 5 minutes before serving.

Sweet Baby Carrots

Servings: 4

Cooking Time: 25 Minutes

Ingredients:

- 1 tbsp of brown sugar
- 2 cups of baby carrots
- 1/2 tbsp. of melted butter
- Black pepper and salt

Directions:

1. Mix butter, sugar, pepper, carrot, and salt in a bowl.
2. Transfer the mix to the PowerXL Air Fryer Grill pan
3. Set the PowerXL Air Fryer Grill to air fry function.
4. Cook for 10 minutes at 350ºF
5. Serve immediately

Nutrition Info: Calories: 77kcal, Fat: 3g, Carb: 15g, Proteins: 3g

Blue Cheese Salad And Beets

Servings: 5

Cooking Time: 30 Minutes

Ingredients:

- 1 tbsp of olive oil
- Black pepper and salt
- 6 beets
- 1/4 cup of blue cheese

Directions:

1. Set the beets on the PowerXL Air Fryer Grill pan.
2. Set the PowerXL Air Fryer Grill to air fry function.
3. Set timer to 15 minutes.
4. Cook at 350ºF
5. Transfer it to a plate.
6. Add pepper, blue cheese, oil, and salt.
7. Serve immediately

Nutrition Info: Calories: 110kcal, Fat: 11g, Carb: 4g, Proteins: 5g

Easy Cinnamon Squash

Servings: 2

Cooking Time: 15 Minutes

Ingredients:

- 1 medium acorn squash, halved crosswise and deseeded
- 1 teaspoon coconut oil
- 1 teaspoon light brown sugar
- Few dashes of ground cinnamon
- Few dashes of ground nutmeg

Directions:

1. On a clean work surface, rub the cut sides of the acorn squash with coconut oil. Scatter with the cinnamon, nutmeg, and brown sugar.
2. Put the squash halves in the air fry basket, cut-side up.
3. Place the basket on the air fry position.
4. Select Air Fry, set temperature to 325ºF (163ºC), and set time to 15 minutes.
5. When cooking is complete, the squash halves should be just tender when pierced in the center with a paring knife. Remove the basket from the air fryer grill. Rest for 5 to 10 minutes and serve warm.

Golden Garlicky Potatoes

Servings: 4
Cooking Time: 15 To 20 Minutes

Ingredients:

- 2 cup sliced frozen potatoes, thawed
- 3 cloves garlic, minced
- Pinch salt
- Freshly ground black pepper, to taste
- ¾ cup heavy cream

Directions:

1. Toss the potatoes with the salt, garlic, and black pepper in a baking pan until evenly coated. Pour the heavy cream over the top.
2. Place the pan on the bake position.
3. Select Bake, set temperature to 380ºF (193ºC), and set time to 15 minutes.
4. When cooking is complete, the potatoes should be tender and the top golden brown. Check for doneness and bake for another 5 minutes if needed. Remove from the air fryer grill and serve hot.

Fast Lemony Wax Beans

Servings: 4
Cooking Time: 12 Minutes

Ingredients:

- 2 pounds (907 g) wax beans
- 2 tablespoons extra-virgin olive oil
- Salt and freshly ground black pepper, to taste
- Juice of ½ lemon, for serving

Directions:

1. Line a baking sheet with aluminum foil.
2. Toss the wax beans with the olive oil in a large bowl. Lightly season with pepper and salt.
3. Spread out the wax beans on the sheet pan.
4. Place the baking sheet on the toast position.
5. Select Toast, set temperature to 400ºF (205ºC), and set time to 12 minutes.
6. When done, the beans will be caramelized and tender. Remove from the air fryer grill to a plate and serve sprinkled with the lemon juice.

Cabbage Wedges With Mozzarella

Servings: 4

Cooking Time: 20 Minutes

Ingredients:

- 4 tablespoons melted butter
- 1 head cabbage, cut into wedges
- 1 cup shredded Parmesan cheese
- Salt and black pepper, to taste
- ½ cup shredded Mozzarella cheese

Directions:

1. Brush the melted butter over the cut sides of cabbage wedges and sprinkle both sides with the Parmesan cheese. Season with salt and pepper to taste.
2. Place the cabbage wedges in the air fry basket.
3. Place the air fry basket on the air fry position.
4. Select Air Fry, set temperature to 380ºF (193ºC), and set time to 20 minutes. Flip the cabbage halfway through the cooking time.
5. When cooking is complete, the cabbage wedges should be lightly browned. Transfer the cabbage wedges to a plate and serve with the Mozzarella cheese sprinkled on top.

Easy Cinnamon Celery Roots

Servings: 4

Cooking Time: 20 Minutes

Ingredients:

- 2 celery roots, peeled and diced
- 1 teaspoon extra-virgin olive oil
- 1 teaspoon butter, melted
- ½ teaspoon ground cinnamon
- Sea salt and freshly ground black pepper, to taste

Directions:

1. Line a baking sheet with aluminum foil.
2. Toss the celery roots with the olive oil in a large bowl until well coated. Transfer them to the prepared baking sheet.
3. Place the baking sheet on the toast position.
4. Select Toast, set temperature to 350ºF (180ºC), and set time to 20 minutes.
5. When done, the celery roots should be very tender. Remove from the air fryer grill to a serving bowl. Stir in the butter and cinnamon and mash them with a potato masher until fluffy.
6. Season with salt and pepper to taste. Serve immediately.

Garlicky-balsamic Asparagus

Servings: 4
Cooking Time: 10 Minutes

Ingredients:

- 1 pound (454 g) asparagus, woody ends trimmed
- 2 tablespoons olive oil
- 1 tablespoon balsamic vinegar
- 2 teaspoons minced garlic
- Salt and freshly ground black pepper, to taste

Directions:

1. In a large shallow bowl, toss the asparagus with the garlic, balsamic vinegar, olive oil, salt, and pepper until thoroughly coated. Put the asparagus in the air fry basket.
2. Place the basket on the toast position.
3. Select Toast, set temperature to 400ºF (205ºC), and set time to 10 minutes. Flip the asparagus with tongs halfway through the cooking time.
4. When cooking is complete, the asparagus should be crispy. Remove the basket from the air fryer grill and serve warm.

Fast Crispy Tofu Sticks

Servings: 4
Cooking Time: 14 Minutes

Ingredients:

- 2 tablespoons olive oil, divided
- ½ cup flour
- ½ cup crushed cornflakes
- Salt and black pepper, to taste
- 14 ounces (397 g) firm tofu, cut into ½-inch-thick strips

Directions:

1. Grease the air fry basket with 1 tablespoon of olive oil.
2. Combine the flour, salt, pepper, and cornflakes on a plate.
3. Dredge the tofu strips in the flour mixture until they are completely coated. Transfer the tofu strips to the greased basket.
4. Drizzle the remaining 1 tablespoon of olive oil over the top of tofu strips.
5. Place the basket on the air fry position.
6. Select Air Fry, set temperature to 360ºF (182ºC), and set time to 14 minutes. Flip the tofu strips halfway through the cooking time.
7. When cooking is complete, the tofu strips should be crispy. Remove from the air fryer grill and serve warm.

Onion Rings

Servings: 3

Cooking Time: 10 Minutes

Ingredients:

- 2 white onions, sliced into rings
- 1 cup flour
- 2 eggs, beaten
- 1 cup breadcrumbs

Directions:

1. Cover the onion rings with flour.
2. Dip in the egg.
3. Dredge with breadcrumbs.
4. Add to the air fryer.
5. Set it to air fry.
6. Cook at 400 degrees F for 10 minutes.

APPETIZERS,SNACKS & DESSERTS

Coconut Shrimp

Servings: 3
Cooking Time: 6 Minutes

Ingredients:

- 9 shrimp, peeled and deveined
- ½ cup flour
- 1 egg
- 1 cup breadcrumbs
- 1 cup coconut flakes

Directions:

1. Coat shrimp with flour.
2. Dip in egg.
3. Dredge with a mixture of breadcrumbs and coconut flakes.
4. Arrange shrimp in the air fryer.
5. Set it to air fry.
6. Cook at 320 degrees F for 6 minutes per side.

Crispy Apple Chips

Servings: 4
Cooking Time: 10 Minutes

Ingredients:

- 4 medium apples (any type will work), cored and thinly sliced
- ¼ teaspoon nutmeg
- ¼ teaspoon cinnamon
- Cooking spray

Directions:

1. Place the apple slices in a large bowl and sprinkle the spices on top. Toss to coat.
2. Put the apple slices in the air fry basket in a single layer and spray them with cooking spray.
3. Place the basket on the air fry position.
4. Select Air Fry, set temperature to 360ºF (182ºC), and set time to 10 minutes. Stir the apple slices halfway through.
5. When cooking is complete, the apple chips should be crispy. Transfer the apple chips to a paper towel-lined plate and rest for 5 minutes before serving.

Crunchy Cinnamon Apple Chips

Servings: 4

Cooking Time: 10 Minutes

Ingredients:

- 2 apples, cored and cut into thin slices
- 2 heaped teaspoons ground cinnamon
- Cooking spray

Directions:

1. Spritz the air fry basket with cooking spray.
2. In a medium bowl, sprinkle the apple slices with the cinnamon. Toss until evenly coated. Spread the coated apple slices on the pan in a single layer.
3. Place the basket on the air fry position.
4. Select Air Fry, set temperature to 350ºF (180ºC) and set time to 10 minutes.
5. After 5 minutes, remove the basket from the air fryer grill. Stir the apple slices and return the basket to the air fryer grill to continue cooking.
6. When cooking is complete, the slices should be until crispy Remove the basket from the air fryer grill and let rest for 5 minutes before serving.

Fast Coconut Pineapple Sticks

Servings: 4

Cooking Time: 10 Minutes

Ingredients:

- ½ fresh pineapple, cut into sticks
- ¼ cup desiccated coconut

Directions:

1. Place the desiccated coconut on a plate and roll the pineapple sticks in the coconut until well coated.
2. Lay the pineapple sticks in the air fry basket.
3. Place the basket on the air fry position.
4. Select Air Fry, set temperature to 400ºF (205ºC), and set time to 10 minutes.
5. When cooking is complete, the pineapple sticks should be crisp-tender.
6. Serve warm.

Simple Bagel

Servings: 4
Cooking Time: 30 Minutes.

Ingredients:

- 1 cup flour
- 1 egg white, beaten
- 3 tsp. salt
- 2 tsp. baking powder
- 1 cup yogurt.

Directions:

1. Add all the ingredients to make the dough.
2. Knead the dough until tacky.
3. Make small balls and roll to give a shape.
4. Sprinkle toppings if required.
5. Preheat the PowerXL Air Fryer Grill to 190ºC or 375ºF and bake for 20-25 minutes.

Nutrition Info: Calories: 152cal, Carbs: 26.5g, Protein: 10g, Fat: 0.3g.

Cream Caramel

Servings: 4
Cooking Time: 25 Minutes

Ingredients:

- 3 tbsp of powdered sugar
- 4 tbsp of caramel
- 2 cups of milk
- 3 tbsp of unsalted butter
- 2 cups custard powder

Directions:

1. Boil sugar and milk over medium heat.
2. Add custard powder.
3. Mix until it thickens.
4. Transfer the mixture to PowerXL Air Fryer Grill pan.
5. Set the PowerXL Air Fryer Grill to air fry function.
6. Cook for 10 minutes at 250ºF.
7. Serve immediately with caramel.

Nutrition Info: Calories: 147kcal, Fat: 5g, Carb: 24g, Proteins: 6g

Simple Sweet Cinnamon Peaches

Servings: 4

Cooking Time: 10 Minutes

Ingredients:

- 2 tablespoons sugar
- ¼ teaspoon ground cinnamon
- 4 peaches, cut into wedges
- Cooking spray

Directions:

1. Spritz the air fry basket with cooking spray.
2. In a large bowl, stir together the sugar and cinnamon. Add the peaches to the bowl and toss to coat evenly.
3. Spread the coated peaches in a single layer in the air fry basket.
4. Place the basket on the air fry position.
5. Select Air Fry, set temperature to 350ºF (180ºC) and set time to 10 minutes.
6. After 5 minutes, remove the basket from the air fryer grill. Use tongs to turn the peaches skin side down. Lightly mist them with cooking spray. Return the basket to the air fryer grill to continue cooking.
7. When cooking is complete, the peaches will be lightly browned and caramelized. Remove the basket from the air fryer grill and let rest for 5 minutes before serving.

Fast Old Bay Chicken Wings

Servings: 4

Cooking Time: 13 Minutes

Ingredients:

- 2 tablespoons Old Bay seasoning
- 2 teaspoons baking powder
- 2 teaspoons salt
- 2 pounds (907 g) chicken wings , patted dry
- Cooking spray

Directions:

1. Combine the Old Bay seasoning, salt, and baking powder in a large zip-top plastic bag. Add the chicken wings, seal, and shake until the wings are thoroughly coated in the seasoning mixture.
2. Lightly spray the air fry basket with cooking spray. Lay the chicken wings in the air fry basket in a single layer and lightly mist them with cooking spray.
3. Place the basket on the air fry position.
4. Select Air Fry, set temperature to 400ºF (205ºC), and set time to 13 minutes. Flip the wings halfway through the cooking time.
5. When cooking is complete, the wings should reach an internal temperature of 165ºF (74ºC) on a meat thermometer. Remove from the air fryer grill to a plate and serve hot.

Cheesy Sausage Balls

Servings: 8

Cooking Time: 10 Minutes

Ingredients:

- 12 ounces (340 g) mild ground sausage
- 1½ cups baking mix
- 1 cup shredded mild Cheddar cheese
- 3 ounces (85 g) cream cheese, at room temperature
- 1 to 2 tablespoons olive oil

Directions:

1. Line the air fry basket with parchment paper. Set aside.
2. Mix together the ground sausage, Cheddar cheese, cream cheese, and baking mix in a large bowl and stir to incorporate.
3. Divide the sausage mixture into 16 equal portions and roll them into 1-inch balls with your hands. Arrange the sausage balls on the parchment, leaving space between each ball. Brush the sausage balls with the olive oil.
4. Place the basket on the air fry position.
5. Select Air Fry, set temperature to 325ºF (163ºC), and set time to 10 minutes. Flip the balls halfway through the cooking time.
6. When cooking is complete, the balls should be firm and lightly browned on both sides. Remove from the air fryer grill to a plate and serve warm.

Gooey Cinnamon S'mores

Servings: 12 S'mores

Cooking Time: 3 Minutes

Ingredients:

- 12 whole cinnamon graham crackers, halved
- 2 (1.55-ounce / 44-g) chocolate bars, cut into 12 pieces
- 12 marshmallows

Directions:

1. Arrange 12 graham cracker squares in the air fry basket in a single layer.
2. Top each square with a piece of chocolate.
3. Place the basket on the bake position.
4. Select Bake, set temperature to 350ºF (180ºC), and set time to 3 minutes.
5. After 2 minutes, remove the basket and place a marshmallow on each piece of melted chocolate. Return the basket to the air fryer grill and continue to cook for another 1 minute.
6. Remove from the air fryer grill to a serving plate.
7. Serve topped with the remaining graham cracker squares

Super Cheesy Sandwiches

Servings: 4 To 8

Cooking Time: 6 Minutes

Ingredients:

- 8 ounces (227 g) Brie
- 8 slices oat nut bread
- 1 large ripe pear, cored and cut into ½-inch-thick slices
- 2 tablespoons butter, melted

Directions:

1. Make the sandwiches: Spread each of 4 slices of bread with ¼ of the Brie. Top the Brie with the pear slices and remaining 4 bread slices.
2. Brush the melted butter lightly on both sides of each sandwich.
3. Arrange the sandwiches in the air fry basket.
4. Place the basket on the bake position.
5. Select Bake, set temperature to 360ºF (182ºC), and set time to 6 minutes.
6. When cooking is complete, the cheese should be melted. Remove the basket from the air fryer grill and serve warm.

Apple Chips

Servings: 2

Cooking Time: 12 Minutes

Ingredients:

- 2 apples, sliced thinly
- 2 teaspoons granulated sugar
- ½ teaspoon cinnamon

Directions:

1. Coat apple slices with sugar and cinnamon.
2. Add these to the air fryer.
3. Choose bake setting.
4. Cook at 350 degrees F for 12 minutes, flipping two to three times.

Avocado Fries With Bacon

Servings: 6

Cooking Time: 10 Minutes

Ingredients:

- 1 avocado, sliced into wedges
- 12 to 15 strips bacon
- Cooking spray

Directions:

1. Wrap the avocado wedges with bacon.
2. Spray with oil.
3. Add to the air fryer.
4. Set it to air fry.
5. Cook at 400 degrees F for 10 minutes.

Grilled Pineapple

Servings: 4

Cooking Time: 10 Minutes

Ingredients:

- 1 pineapple, sliced
- 4 tablespoons butter, melted
- ½ cup brown sugar
- 2 teaspoons cinnamon powder

Directions:

1. Brush pineapple slices with butter.
2. Sprinkle with sugar and cinnamon powder.
3. Air fry at 400 degrees F for 10 minutes.

Easy Turkey Bacon-wrapped Dates

Servings: 16 Appetizers

Cooking Time: 6 Minutes

Ingredients:

- 16 whole dates, pitted
- 16 whole almonds
- 6 to 8 strips turkey bacon, cut in half
- Special Equipment:
- 16 toothpicks, soaked in water for at least 30 minutes

Directions:

1. On a flat work surface, stuff each pitted date with a whole almond.
2. Wrap half slice of bacon around each date and secure it with a toothpick.
3. Place the bacon-wrapped dates in the air fry basket.
4. Place the basket on the air fry position.
5. Select Air Fry, set temperature to 390ºF (199ºC), and set time to 6 minutes.
6. When cooking is complete, transfer the dates to a paper towel-lined plate to drain. Serve hot.

Fast Prosciutto-wrapped Pears

Servings: 8

Cooking Time: 6 Minutes

Ingredients:

- 2 large, ripe Anjou pears
- 4 thin slices Parma prosciutto
- 2 teaspoons aged balsamic vinegar

Directions:

1. Peel the pears. Slice into 8 wedges and cut out the core from each wedge.
2. Cut the prosciutto into 8 long strips. Wrap each pear wedge with a strip of prosciutto. Place the wrapped pears in the sheet pan.
3. Place the pan on the broil position.
4. Select Broil, set temperature to 450ºF (232ºC) and set time to 6 minutes.
5. After 2 or 3 minutes, check the pears. The pears should be turned over if the prosciutto is beginning to crisp up and brown. Return the pan to the air fryer grill and continue cooking.
6. When cooking is complete, remove the pan from the air fryer grill. Drizzle the pears with the balsamic vinegar and serve warm.

Easy Caramelized Peaches

Servings: 4

Cooking Time: 10 To 13 Minutes

Ingredients:

- 2 tablespoons sugar
- ¼ teaspoon ground cinnamon
- 4 peaches, cut into wedges
- Cooking spray

Directions:

1. Toss the peaches with the sugar and cinnamon in a medium bowl until evenly coated.
2. Lightly spray the air fry basket with cooking spray. Place the peaches in the air fry basket in a single layer. Lightly mist the peaches with cooking spray.
3. Place the basket on the air fry position.
4. Select Air Fry, set temperature to 350ºF (180ºC), and set time to 10 minutes.
5. After 5 minutes, remove from the air fryer grill and flip the peaches. Return to the air fryer grill and continue cooking for 5 minutes.
6. When cooking is complete, the peaches should be caramelized. If necessary, continue cooking for 3 minutes. Remove the basket from the air fryer grill. Let the peaches cool for 5 minutes and serve warm.

Dried Salty Almonds

Servings: 4

Cooking Time: 25 Minutes

Ingredients:

- 1 cup raw almonds
- 1 egg white, beaten
- ½ teaspoon coarse sea salt

Directions:

1. Spread the almonds on the sheet pan in an even layer.
2. Place the pan on the bake position.
3. Select Bake, set temperature to 350ºF (180ºC) and set time to 20 minutes.
4. When cooking is complete, the almonds should be lightly browned and fragrant. Remove the pan from the air fryer grill.
5. Coat the almonds with the egg white and sprinkle with the salt. Return the pan to the air fryer grill.
6. Select Bake, set temperature to 350ºF (180ºC) and set time to 5 minutes.
7. When cooking is complete, the almonds should be dried. Cool completely before serving.

Pineapple Bagel Brûlées

Servings: 8

Cooking Time: 20 Minutes.

Ingredients:

- 4 thin bagels
- 4 tsp. brown sugar
- 3/4 cup low-fat cream cheese
- 8 slices pineapples
- 3 tbsp. almonds, toasted

Directions:

1. Preheat the PowerXL Air Fryer Grill at 220ºC or 425ºF.
2. Bake the pineapple slices with brown sugar sprinkled on top.
3. Toast bagels, and apply cream cheese, almonds, and baked pineapples.

Nutrition Info: Calories: 157cal, Carbs: 22.9g, Protein: 5.6g, Fat: 6.4g.

Cinnamon Apple Wedges With Yogurt

Servings: 4

Cooking Time: 12 Minutes

Ingredients:

- 2 medium apples, cored and sliced into ¼-inch wedges
- 1 teaspoon canola oil
- 2 teaspoons peeled and grated fresh ginger
- ½ teaspoon ground cinnamon
- ½ cup low-fat Greek vanilla yogurt, for serving

Directions:

1. In a large bowl, toss the apple wedges with the cinnamon, ginger, and canola oil until evenly coated. Put the apple wedges in the air fry basket.
2. Place the basket on the air fry position.
3. Select Air Fry, set temperature to 360ºF (182ºC), and set time to 12 minutes.
4. When cooking is complete, the apple wedges should be crisp-tender. Remove the apple wedges from the air fryer grill and serve drizzled with the yogurt.

Pumpkin Spice Bagels

Servings: 1

Cooking Time: 30minutes

Ingredients:

- 1 egg
- 1 cup flour
- 1/2 tsp. pumpkin spice
- 1/2 cup Greek yogurt

Directions:

1. Create a dough with flour, pie spice, yogurt, and pumpkin in a stand mixer.
2. Shape the dough into a few ropes and make bagels.
3. Apply egg and water mixture over the bagels.
4. Preheat the PowerXL Air Fryer Grill to 190ºC or 375ºF and bake for 20-25 minutes.

Nutrition Info: Calories: 183, Carbs: 32.7g, Protein: 9.4g, Fat: 2g.

Wild Blueberry Bagels

Servings: 1

Cooking Time: 5minutes.

Ingredients:

- 1 bagel
- 1 tbsp. low-fat cream cheese
- 2 tbsp. frozen wild blueberries
- 1/4 tsp. cinnamon

Directions:

1. Preheat the PowerXL Air Fryer Grill to 190ºC or 375ºF
2. Toast the bagel for 3-5 minutes.
3. Spread cream cheese, add blueberry toppings, and cinnamon.

Nutrition Info: Calories: 155cal, Carbs: 25g, Protein: 6g, Fat:3.5g.

Roasted Garlic Dip

Servings: 6

Cooking Time: 20 Minutes

Ingredients:

- 1 head garlic
- ½ tablespoon olive oil

Directions:

1. Slice the top off the garlic.
2. Drizzle with the olive oil.
3. Add to the air fryer.
4. Set it to roast.
5. Cook at 390 degrees F for 20 minutes.
6. Peel the garlic.
7. Transfer to a food processor.
8. Pulse until smooth.

Choco Hazelnut Croissant

Servings: 2

Cooking Time: 10 Minutes

Ingredients:

- 1 oz. canned crescent rolls
- 8 teaspoons chocolate hazelnut spread

Directions:

1. Separate crescent dough into triangles.
2. Spread top with chocolate hazelnut spread.
3. Roll up the triangles to form a crescent shape.
4. Place these in the air fryer.
5. Select bake setting.
6. Cook at 320 degrees F for 8 to 10 minutes or until golden.

Golden Lemon Pepper Wings

Servings: 10

Cooking Time: 24 Minutes

Ingredients:

- 2 pounds (907 g) chicken wings
- 4½ teaspoons salt-free lemon pepper seasoning
- 1½ teaspoons baking powder
- 1½ teaspoons kosher salt

Directions:

1. In a large bowl, toss together all the ingredients until well coated. Place the wings on the sheet pan, making sure they don't crowd each other too much.
2. Slide the pan into the air fryer grill.
3. Select Air Fry, set temperature to 375ºF (190ºC) and set time to 24 minutes.
4. After 12 minutes, remove the pan from the air fryer grill. Use tongs to turn the wings over. Rotate the pan and return the pan to the air fryer grill to continue cooking.
5. When cooking is complete, the wings should be dark golden brown and a bit charred in places. Remove the pan from the air fryer grill and let rest for 5 minutes before serving.

Cinnamon Softened Apples

Servings: 4

Cooking Time: 12 Minutes

Ingredients:

- 1 cup packed light brown sugar
- 2 teaspoons ground cinnamon
- 2 medium Granny Smith apples, peeled and diced

Directions:

1. Thoroughly combine the cinnamon and brown sugar in a medium bowl.
2. Add the apples to the bowl and stir until well coated. Transfer the apples to a baking pan.
3. Place the pan on the bake position.
4. Select Bake, set temperature to 350ºF (180ºC), and set time to 12 minutes.
5. After about 9 minutes, stir the apples and bake for an additional 3 minutes. When cooking is complete, the apples should be softened.
6. Serve warm.

Bacon Onion Rings

Servings: 4
Cooking Time: 10 Minutes

Ingredients:

- 2 white onions, sliced into rings
- 1 tablespoon hot sauce
- 10 bacon slices

Directions:

1. Coat onion rings with hot sauce.
2. Wrap each onion ring with bacon.
3. Add to the air fryer.
4. Set it to air fry.
5. Cook at 370 degrees F for 5 minutes per side.

Southwestern Waffles

Servings: 1
Cooking Time: 10minutes.

Ingredients:

- 1 egg, fried
- 1/4 avocado, chopped
- 1 frozen waffle
- 1 tbsp. salsa

Directions:

1. Preheat the PowerXL Air Fryer Grill to 200ºC or 400ºF.
2. Bake the waffles for 5-7 minutes.
3. Add avocado, fried eggs, and fresh salsa as toppings.

Nutrition Info: Calories: 207cal, Carbs: 17g, Protein: 9g, Fat: 12g.

Grilled Cheese Sandwich

Servings: 1

Cooking Time: 8 Minutes

Ingredients:

- 2 slices bread
- 1 tablespoon butter
- 2 slices cheddar cheese

Directions:

1. Spread one side of bread slices with butter.
2. Place the cheese between the two bread slices.
3. Choose grill setting in your air fryer.
4. Cook at 350 degrees F for 5 minutes.
5. Flip and cook for another 3 minutes.

Caramelized Peaches

Servings: 2

Cooking Time: 15 Minutes

Ingredients:

- 1 lb. peaches, sliced in half
- 1 tablespoon maple syrup
- ½ tablespoon coconut sugar
- ¼ teaspoon cinnamon powder

Directions:

1. Brush peaches with maple syrup.
2. Sprinkle with coconut sugar and cinnamon.
3. Cook in the air fryer at 350 degrees F for 15 minutes.

Golden Egg Bagels

Servings: 8

Cooking Time: 20 Minutes.

Ingredients:

- 2 eggs
- 4 tsp. dry yeast
- 4-5 cups all-purpose flour
- 1 tbsp. canola oil and kosher salt
- 1-1/2 tbsp. sugar

Directions:

1. Whisk eggs, sugar, yeast, lukewarm, water, and oil. Add flour and salt to prepare the dough.
2. Make a long rope with the dough, locking both ends.
3. Preheat the PowerXL Air Fryer Grill to 200ºC or 400ºF.
4. Boil bagels in sugar and salt for 45 seconds.
5. Drain bagels, brush with egg white and bake for 15-20 mins.

Nutrition Info: Calories: 164cal, Carbs: 28.4g, Protein: 6.6g, Fat: 2.1g.

Spicy -sweet Toasted Walnuts

Servings: 4 Cups

Cooking Time: 15 Minutes

Ingredients:

- 1 pound (454 g) walnut halves and pieces
- ½ cup granulated sugar
- 3 tablespoons vegetable oil
- 1 teaspoon cayenne pepper
- ½ teaspoon fine salt

Directions:

1. Soak the walnuts in a large bowl with boiling water for a minute or two. Drain the walnuts. Stir in the oil, sugar and cayenne pepper to coat well. Spread the walnuts in a single layer on the sheet pan.
2. Place the pan on the toast position.
3. Select Toast, set temperature to 325ºF (163ºC) and set time to 15 minutes.
4. After 7 or 8 minutes, remove the pan from the air fryer grill. Stir the nuts. Return the pan to the air fryer grill and continue cooking, check frequently.
5. When cooking is complete, the walnuts should be dark golden brown. Remove the pan from the air fryer grill. Sprinkle the nuts with the salt and let cool. Serve.

Baked Apples & Raisins

Servings: 4
Cooking Time: 20 Minutes
Ingredients:

- 4 apples, sliced
- 6 teaspoons raisins
- 2 teaspoons walnuts, chopped
- 2 teaspoons honey
- ½ teaspoon cinnamon powder

Directions:

1. Mix all the ingredients in a small baking pan.
2. Place inside the air fryer.
3. Set it to bake.
4. Cook at 350 degrees F for 15 minutes.
5. Stir and cook for another 5 minutes.

Pumpkin Seeds

Servings: 6
Cooking Time: 25 Minutes
Ingredients:

- 2 cups pumpkin seeds
- Water
- 1 ½ tablespoons butter
- ½ teaspoon garlic salt

Directions:

1. Add pumpkin seeds to a pot filled with water.
2. Bring to a boil
3. Drain the seeds.
4. Let cool for 5 minutes.
5. Toss pumpkin seeds in butter.
6. Season with garlic salt.
7. Add to the air fryer.
8. Set it to air fry.
9. Cook at 360 degrees F for 15 minutes, shaking once.

Apple Slices Wedges With Apricots

Servings: 4

Cooking Time: 15 To 18 Minutes

Ingredients:

- 4 large apples, peeled and sliced into 8 wedges
- 2 tablespoons olive oil
- ½ cup dried apricots, chopped
- 1 to 2 tablespoons sugar
- ½ teaspoon ground cinnamon

Directions:

1. Toss the apple wedges with the olive oil in a mixing bowl until well coated.
2. Place the apple wedges in the air fry basket.
3. Place the basket on the air fry position.
4. Select Air Fry, set temperature to 350ºF (180ºC), and set time to 15 minutes.
5. After about 12 minutes, remove from the air fryer grill. Sprinkle with the dried apricots and air fry for another 3 minutes.
6. Meanwhile, thoroughly combine the cinnamon and sugar in a small bowl.
7. Remove the apple wedges from the air fryer grill to a plate. Serve sprinkled with the sugar mixture.

Cheesy Pepperoni Pizza Bites

Servings: 8

Cooking Time: 12 Minutes

Ingredients:

- 1 cup finely shredded Mozzarella cheese
- ½ cup chopped pepperoni
- ¼ cup Marinara sauce
- 1 (8-ounce / 227-g) can crescent roll dough
- All-purpose flour, for dusting

Directions:

1. In a small bowl, stir together the cheese, pepperoni, and Marinara sauce.
2. Lay the dough on a lightly floured work surface. Separate it into 4 rectangles. Firmly pinch the perforations together and pat the dough pieces flat.
3. Divide the cheese mixture evenly between the rectangles and spread it out over the dough, leaving a ¼-inch border. Roll a rectangle up tightly, starting with the short end. Pinch the edge down to seal the roll. Repeat with the remaining rolls.
4. Slice the rolls into 4 or 5 even slices. Place the slices on the sheet pan, leaving a few inches between each slice.
5. Place the pan on the toast position.
6. Select Toast, set temperature to 350ºF (180ºC) and set time to 12 minutes.
7. After 6 minutes, rotate the pan and continue cooking.
8. When cooking is complete, the rolls will be golden brown with crisp edges. Remove the pan from the air fryer grill. Serve hot.

Crispy Carrot Chips

Servings: 4
Cooking Time: 10 Minutes

Ingredients:

- 4 to 5 medium carrots, trimmed and thinly sliced
- 1 tablespoon olive oil, plus more for greasing
- 1 teaspoon seasoned salt

Directions:

1. Toss the carrot slices with 1 tablespoon of olive oil and salt in a medium bowl until thoroughly coated.
2. Grease the air fry basket with the olive oil. Place the carrot slices in the greased pan.
3. Place the basket on the air fry position.
4. Select Air Fry, set temperature to 390ºF (199ºC), and set time to 10 minutes. Stir the carrot slices halfway through the cooking time.
5. When cooking is complete, the chips should be crisp-tender. Remove the basket from the air fryer grill and allow to cool for 5 minutes before serving.

Potato Tots

Servings: 4
Cooking Time: 8 Minutes

Ingredients:

- 12 potato tots
- 12 bacon strips

Directions:

1. Wrap the potato tots with bacon strips.
2. Add to the air fryer.
3. Set it to air fry.
4. Cook at 400 degrees F for 8 minutes, turning once or twice.

Cinnamon Banana

Servings: 2

Cooking Time: 5 Minutes

Ingredients:

- 2 bananas, sliced
- ¼ teaspoon cinnamon
- ½ teaspoon brown sugar
- 1 tablespoon granola

Directions:

1. Toss the ingredients in a bowl.
2. Pour into a small baking pan.
3. Air fry at 400 degrees F for 5 minutes.

Sago Payasam

Servings: 5

Cooking Time: 25 Minutes

Ingredients:

- 3 tbsp of powdered sugar
- 2 cups of milk
- 2 tbsp of custard powder
- 3 tbsp of unsalted butter
- 2 cups of soaked sago

Directions:

1. Put sugar and milk in a pan and boil over medium heat.
2. Add custard powder and sago.
3. Mix until it thickens
4. Transfer the mixture to the PowerXL Air Fryer Grill pan.
5. Set the PowerXL Air Fryer Grill to air fry function.
6. Cook for 10 minutes at 250ºF.

Nutrition Info: Calories: 317kcal, Fat: 2g, Carb: 36g, Proteins: 7g

POULTRY RECIPES

Fast Crispy Chicken Skin

Servings: 4

Cooking Time: 6 Minutes

Ingredients:

- 1 pound (454 g) chicken skin, cut into slices
- 1 teaspoon melted butter
- ½ teaspoon crushed chili flakes
- 1 teaspoon dried dill
- Salt and ground black pepper, to taste

Directions:

1. Combine all the ingredients in a large bowl. Toss to coat the chicken skin well.
2. Transfer the skin in the air fry basket.
3. Place the basket on the air fry position.
4. Select Air Fry. Set temperature to 360ºF (182ºC) and set time to 6 minutes. Stir the skin halfway through.
5. When cooking is complete, the skin should be crispy.
6. Serve immediately.

Air Fried Turkey Breast With Basil

Servings: 4

Cooking Time: 1hour 10 Minutes

Ingredients:

- 2 pounds turkey breasts, bone-in skin-on
- 2 tbsps olive oil
- Coarse sea salt and ground black pepper, to taste
- 1 tsp fresh basil leaves, chopped
- 2 tbsp lemon zest, grated

Directions:

1. Preheat the PowerXL Air Fryer Grill by selecting air fry mode
2. Adjust the temperature to 330ºF, set time to 5 minutes
3. Rub olive on all sides of the turkey breast
4. Sprinkle with salt, pepper, lemon zest, and basil
5. Arrange on the PowerXL grill Pizza rack
6. Transfer to the PowerXL Air Fryer Grill
7. Air fry for 30 minutes.
8. Flip and air fry for another 28 minutes.
9. Enjoy!

Nutrition Info: Calories: 390kcal, Fat: 24g, Carb: 2g, Proteins: 41g

Shredded Chicken Sandwich

Servings: 2

Cooking Time: 25 Minutes

Ingredients:

- Shredded chicken
- Mayo
- Lettuce
- Salt and pepper
- 2 slices of whole-grain bread

Directions:

1. Toast bread with butter in the PowerXL Air Fryer Grill.
2. Mix up all the other ingredients until smooth.
3. Cut the slices into halves and fill it up with the mixture.

Nutrition Info: Calories: 368kcal, Carbs: 51g, Protein: 25g, Fat: 7.2g.

Strawberry-glazed Turkey Breast

Servings: 2
Cooking Time: 37 Minutes

Ingredients:

- 2 pounds (907 g) turkey breast
- 1 tablespoon olive oil
- Salt and ground black pepper, to taste
- 1 cup fresh strawberries

Directions:

1. Rub the turkey bread with olive oil on a clean work surface, then sprinkle with salt and ground black pepper.
2. Transfer the turkey in the air fry basket and spritz with cooking spray.
3. Place the basket on the air fry position.
4. Select Air Fry. Set temperature to 375ºF (190ºC) and set time to 30 minutes. Flip the turkey breast halfway through.
5. Meanwhile, put the strawberries in a food processor and pulse until smooth.
6. When cooking is complete, spread the puréed strawberries over the turkey and fry for 7 more minutes.
7. Serve immediately.

Fast Cajun Chicken Drumsticks

Servings: 5
Cooking Time: 18 Minutes

Ingredients:

- 1 tablespoon olive oil
- 10 chicken drumsticks
- 1½ tablespoons Cajun seasoning
- Salt and ground black pepper, to taste

Directions:

1. Grease the air fry basket with olive oil.
2. On a clean work surface, rub the chicken drumsticks with salt, Cajun seasoning, and ground black pepper.
3. Arrange the seasoned chicken drumsticks in the air fry basket.
4. Place the basket on the air fry position.
5. Select Air Fry. Set temperature to 390ºF (199ºC) and set time to 18 minutes. Flip the drumsticks halfway through.
6. When cooking is complete, the drumsticks should be lightly browned.
7. Remove the chicken drumsticks from the air fryer grill. Serve immediately.

Crispy Duck Leg Quarters

Servings: 4

Cooking Time: 45 Minutes

Ingredients:

- 4 (½-pound / 227-g) skin-on duck leg quarters
- 2 medium garlic cloves, minced
- ½ teaspoon salt
- ½ teaspoon ground black pepper

Directions:

1. Spritz the air fry basket with cooking spray.
2. On a clean work surface, rub the duck leg quarters with garlic, salt, and black pepper.
3. Arrange the leg quarters in the air fry basket and spritz with cooking spray.
4. Place the basket on the air fry position.
5. Select Air Fry. Set temperature to 300ºF (150ºC) and set time to 30 minutes.
6. After 30 minutes, remove the basket from the air fryer grill. Flip the leg quarters. Increase temperature to 375ºF (190ºC) and set time to 15 minutes. Return the basket to the air fryer grill and continue cooking.
7. When cooking is complete, the leg quarters should be well browned and crispy.
8. Remove the duck leg quarters from the air fryer grill and allow to cool for 10 minutes before serving.

Simple Turkey Breast

Servings: 5

Cooking Time: 1 Hour

Ingredients:

- 3 lb. bone-in turkey breast
- Salt and black pepper, as required
- 1 tbsp olive oil

Directions:

1. Preheat the PowerXL Air Fryer Grill by selecting Air Fry mode
2. Adjust the temperature to 360ºF, set time to 5 minutes
3. Season the turkey with salt and pepper
4. Rub with olive oil
5. Arrange on the PowerXL grill Pizza rack
6. Transfer to the PowerXL Air Fryer Grill
7. Air fry for 20 minutes
8. Flip and air fry for an additional 20 minutes
9. Enjoy

Nutrition Info: Calories: 213kcal, Fat: 22g, Carb: 1g, Proteins: 13g

Buttermilk Brined Turkey Breast

Servings: 8

Cooking Time: 35 Minutes

Ingredients:

- 3-1/2 pounds boneless, skinless turkey breast
- 3/4 cup brine from a can of olives
- 1 fresh rosemary sprig
- 2 fresh thyme sprigs
- 1/2 cup buttermilk

Directions:

1. Combine all the ingredients.
2. Add the turkey and pour into a sealable bag
3. Leave to marinate for 12 hours in the refrigerator
4. Preheat the PowerXL Air Fryer Grill by selecting Air fry mode
5. Adjust the temperature to 350ºF, set time to 5 minutes
6. Arrange on the PowerXL grill baking tray
7. Transfer to the PowerXL Air Fryer Grill
8. Air fry for 20 minutes, flip halfway done
9. Enjoy

Nutrition Info: Calories: 215kcal, Fat: 3g, Carb: 8g, Proteins: 32g

Air-fried Chicken Wings

Servings: 4

Cooking Time: 15 Minutes

Ingredients:

- 1 tablespoon olive oil
- 8 whole chicken wings
- Chicken seasoning or rub, to taste
- 1 teaspoon garlic powder
- Freshly ground black pepper, to taste

Directions:

1. Grease the air fry basket with olive oil.
2. On a clean work surface, rub the chicken wings with chicken seasoning and rub, garlic powder, and ground black pepper.
3. Arrange the well-coated chicken wings in the air fry basket.
4. Place the basket on the air fry position.
5. Select Air Fry. Set temperature to 400ºF (205ºC) and set time to 15 minutes. Flip the chicken wings halfway through.
6. When cooking is complete, the internal temperature of the chicken wings should reach at least 165ºF (74ºC).
7. Remove the chicken wings from the air fryer grill. Serve immediately.

Marmalade Balsamic Glaze D Duck Breasts

Servings: 4

Cooking Time: 13 Minutes

Ingredients:

- 4 (6-ounce / 170-g) skin-on duck breasts
- 1 teaspoon salt
- ¼ cup orange marmalade
- 1 tablespoon white balsamic vinegar
- ¾ teaspoon ground black pepper

Directions:

1. Cut 10 slits into the skin of the duck breasts, then sprinkle with salt on both sides.
2. Place the breasts in the air fry basket, skin side up.
3. Place the basket on the air fry position.
4. Select Air Fry. Set temperature to 400ºF (205ºC) and set time to 10 minutes.
5. Meanwhile, combine the remaining ingredients in a small bowl. Stir to mix well.
6. When cooking is complete, brush the duck skin with the marmalade mixture. Flip the breast and air fry for 3 more minutes or until the skin is crispy and the breast is well browned.
7. Serve immediately.

Baked Whole Chicken

Servings: 2 To 4

Cooking Time: 1 Hour

Ingredients:

- ½ cup melted butter
- 3 tablespoons garlic, minced
- Salt, to taste
- 1 teaspoon ground black pepper
- 1 (1-pound / 454-g) whole chicken

Directions:

1. Combine the butter with salt, garlic, and ground black pepper in a small bowl.
2. Brush the butter mixture over the whole chicken, then place the chicken in the air fry basket, skin side down.
3. Place the basket on the bake position.
4. Select Bake, set temperature to 350ºF (180ºC) and set time to 60 minutes. Flip the chicken halfway through.
5. When cooking is complete, an instant-read thermometer inserted in the thickest part of the chicken should register at least 165 ºF (74 ºC).
6. Remove the chicken from the air fryer grill and allow to cool for 15 minutes before serving.

FAST AND EASY EVERYDAY FAVORITES

Baked Grits

Servings: about 4 Cups

Cooking Time: 1 Hour 5 Minutes

Ingredients:

- 1 cup grits or polenta (not instant or quick cook)
- 2 cups milk
- 2 cups chicken or vegetable stock
- 2 tablespoons unsalted butter, cut into 4 pieces
- 1 teaspoon kosher salt or ½ teaspoon fine salt

Directions:

1. Add the grits to the baking pan. Stir in the milk, stock, butter, and salt.
2. Place the pan on the bake position. Select Bake, set the temperature to 325ºF (163ºC), and set the time for 1 hour and 5 minutes.
3. After 15 minutes, remove the pan from the air fryer grill and stir the polenta. Return the pan to the air fryer grill and continue cooking.
4. After 30 minutes, remove the pan again and stir the polenta again. Return the pan to the air fryer grill and continue cooking for 15 to 20 minutes, or until the polenta is soft and creamy and the liquid is absorbed.
5. When done, remove the pan from the air fryer air fryer grill.
6. Serve immediately.

Breakfast Pizza

Servings: 5

Cooking Time: 15 Minutes

Ingredients:

- 1 pound of bacon
- 8 ounces of crescent dinner rolls
- 1 cup of cheddar cheese
- 6 eggs

Directions:

1. Place the rolls on the pizza pan.
2. Mix cheese, eggs, and bacon in a bowl.
3. Pour the mixture over the crust.
4. Place the pan in the PowerXL Air Fryer Grill.
5. Set the PowerXL Air Fryer Grill to pizza function.
6. Cook for 15 minutes at 370ºF.
7. Serve immediately

Nutrition Info: Calories: 311kcal, Fat: 11g, Carb: 43g, Proteins: 15g

Pepperoni Pizza

Servings: 8

Cooking Time: 30 Minutes

Ingredients:

- Pepperoni, sliced
- 1 cup pizza sauce
- 1 cup mozzarella cheese
- Readymade pizza dough
- Parmesan cheese, grated

Directions:

1. Arrange toppings on pizza dough.
2. Preheat the PowerXL Air Fryer Grill to 177ºC or 350ºF.
3. Bake for 25 minutes.

Nutrition Info: Calories: 235kcal, Carbs: 35.6g, Protein: 11g, Fat: 11g.

Chicken Focaccia Bread Sandwiches

Servings: 6
Cooking Time: 15 Minutes

Ingredients:

- Flatbread or Focaccia, halved
- 2 cups chicken, sliced
- Fresh basil leaves
- 1 cup sweet pepper, roasted

Directions:

1. Roast the chicken at 177ºC or 350ºF in the PowerXL Air Fryer Grill for 25 to 30 minutes.
2. Spread mayonnaise on the bread and put the remaining ingredients on top.

Nutrition Info: Calories: 263cal, Carbs: 26.9g, Protein: 19g, Fat: 10g.

Powerxl Air Fryer Grill-baked Grilled Cheese

Servings: 1
Cooking Time: 10 Minutes

Ingredients:

- 2 slices bread
- 1-2 tsp. mayonnaise
- 2-3 tsp. cheddar cheese
- Fresh spinach

Directions:

1. Preheat the PowerXL Air Fryer Grill to 200ºC or 400ºF.
2. Spread mayonnaise and cheese on the bread.
3. Bake for 5-7 minutes. Add the spinach.

Nutrition Info: Calories: 353kcal, Carbs: 42.1g, Protein: 18.9g, Fat: 7.8g.

Powerxl Air Fryer Grill Pizza Sandwiches

Servings: 1

Cooking Time: 5minutes

Ingredients:

- 1 French bread sandwich roll, sliced
- 5 tsp. pizza sauce
- 15-20 slices pepperoni
- 1 cup mozzarella cheese, shredded

Directions:

1. Preheat the PowerXL Air Fryer Grill to 250ºC or 482ºF.
2. Spread pizza sauce on the bread.
3. Add toppings, cheese, and pepperoni on each slice of bread.
4. Toast it until the cheese melts.

Nutrition Info: Calories: 752.1kcal, Carbs: 33.5 g, Protein: 35.2 g, Fat: 15.7g.

Air-fried Okra Chips

Servings: 6

Cooking Time: 16 Minutes

Ingredients:

- 2 pounds (907 g) fresh okra pods, cut into 1-inch pieces
- 2 tablespoons canola oil
- 1 teaspoon coarse sea salt

Directions:

1. Stir the salt and oil in a bowl to mix well. Add the okra and toss to coat well. Place the okra in the air fry basket.
2. Place the basket on the air fry position.
3. Select Air Fry, set temperature to 400ºF (205ºC) and set time to 16 minutes. Flip the okra at least three times during cooking.
4. When cooked, the okra should be lightly browned. Remove from the air fryer grill.
5. Serve immediately.

Cheesy Eggplant Hoagies

Servings: 3 Hoagies

Cooking Time: 12 Minutes

Ingredients:

- 6 peeled eggplant slices (about ½ inch thick and 3 inches in diameter)
- ¼ cup jarred pizza sauce
- 6 tablespoons grated Parmesan cheese
- 3 Italian sub rolls, split open lengthwise, warmed
- Cooking spray

Directions:

1. Spritz the air fry basket with cooking spray.
2. Arrange the eggplant slices in the basket and spritz with cooking spray.
3. Place the basket on the air fry position.
4. Select Air Fry, set temperature to 350ºF (180ºC) and set time to 10 minutes. Flip the slices halfway through the cooking time.
5. When cooked, the eggplant slices should be lightly wilted and tender.
6. Divide and spread the pizza sauce and cheese on top of the eggplant slice
7. Place the basket on the air fry position.
8. Select Air Fry, set temperature to 375ºF (190ºC) and set time to 2 minutes. When cooked, the cheese will be melted.
9. Assemble each sub roll with two slices of eggplant and serve immediately.

Golden Chocolate And Coconut Macaroons

Servings: 24

Cooking Time: 8 Minutes

Ingredients:

- 3 large egg whites, at room temperature
- ¼ teaspoon salt
- ¾ cup granulated white sugar
- 4½ tablespoons unsweetened cocoa powder
- 2¼ cups unsweetened shredded coconut

Directions:

1. Line the air fry basket with parchment paper.
2. Whisk the egg whites with salt in a large bowl with a hand mixer on high speed until stiff peaks form.
3. Whisk in the sugar with the hand mixer on high speed until the mixture is thick. Mix in the cocoa powder and coconut.
4. Scoop 2 tablespoons of the mixture and shape the mixture in a ball. Repeat with remaining mixture to make 24 balls in total.
5. Arrange the balls in a single layer in the air fry basket and leave a little space between each two balls.
6. Place the basket on the air fry position.
7. Select Air Fry, set temperature to 375ºF (190ºC) and set time to 8 minutes.
8. When cooking is complete, the balls should be golden brown.
9. Serve immediately.

Roasted Filet Mignon

Servings: 2

Cooking Time: 30 Minutes

Ingredients:

- 10 ounces filet mignon
- 1 tbsp. Italian herbs, chopped
- Salt & pepper
- 2 tbsp. olive oil

Directions:

1. Preheat the PowerXL Air Fryer Grill to 200ºC or 400ºF.
2. Mix all the seasonings and oil, and rub the mixture on the steak.
3. Roast it for 30 minutes.

Nutrition Info: Calories: 267kcal, Protein: 26g, Fat: 17g

Roasted Spaghetti Squash

Servings: 4
Cooking Time: 30 Minutes

Ingredients:

- 1 ripe squash
- Salt & pepper

Directions:

1. Preheat the PowerXL Air Fryer Grill to 150ºC or 300ºF.
2. Prick the outside of the cleaned squash with a fork.
3. Roast it for 10 minutes.
4. Cut the roasted squash and scrape out the strands.
5. Sprinkle salt and pepper and serve.

Nutrition Info: Calories: 42kcal, Carbs: 3g, Protein: 1g, Fat: 0.5g,

Cheesy Bread

Servings: 4
Cooking Time: 20 Minutes

Ingredients:

- 4 cloves of garlic
- 1 cup of mozzarella cheese
- 8 slices of bread
- 6 tsp of sun-dried tomatoes
- 5 tbsp of melted butter

Directions:

1. Place the bread slices on a flat surface.
2. Put butter on it, garlic, and tomato paste.
3. Add cheese
4. Place the bread on the PowerXL Air Fryer Grill pan.
5. Set the PowerXL Air Fryer Grill to toast/bagel function.
6. Cook for 8 minutes a 350ºF.

Nutrition Info: Calories: 226kcal, Fat: 8g, Carb: 32g, Proteins: 8g

Garlic Bread

Servings: 4
Cooking Time: 20 Minutes

Ingredients:

- 4 pieces baguette, cut in half
- Mint leaves, chopped
- 2-3 tsp. butter
- 2-3 garlic cloves, minced

Directions:

1. Mix butter, mint, and garlic.
2. Spread mixture on every slice.
3. Bake at 200C or 400F in the PowerXL Air Fryer Grill for 5-6 minutes

Nutrition Info: Calories: 160kcal, Carbs: 18g, Protein: 3.6g, Fat: 7.1g.

Steak With Mashed Cauliflower

Servings: 2
Cooking Time: 12 Minutes

Ingredients:

- 2 rib eye steaks
- Salt and pepper to taste
- 2 tablespoons butter
- 2 cups cauliflower florets, roasted
- ¼ cup almond milk

Directions:

1. Choose grill setting in your air fryer.
2. Set it to 400 degrees F.
3. Sprinkle both sides of steak with salt and pepper.
4. Add the steaks to the air fryer.
5. Cook for 12 minutes, flipping halfway through.
6. Add cauliflower florets to a food processor.
7. Stir in almond milk, salt and pepper.
8. Pulse until smooth.
9. Serve steaks with mashed cauliflower.

Golden Avocado And Tomato Egg Rolls

Servings: 5

Cooking Time: 5 Minutes

Ingredients:

- 10 egg roll wrappers
- 3 avocados, peeled and pitted
- 1 tomato, diced
- Salt and ground black pepper, to taste
- Cooking spray

Directions:

1. Spritz the air fry basket with cooking spray.
2. Put the avocados and tomato in a food processor. Sprinkle with salt and ground black pepper. Pulse to mix and coarsely mash until smooth.
3. Unfold the wrappers on a clean work surface, then divide the mixture in the center of each wrapper. Roll the wrapper up and press to seal.
4. Transfer the rolls to the basket and spritz with cooking spray.
5. Place the basket on the air fry position.
6. Select Air Fry, set temperature to 350ºF (180ºC) and set time to 5 minutes. Flip the rolls halfway through the cooking time.
7. When cooked, the rolls should be golden brown.
8. Serve immediately.

Easy Air-fried Edamame

Servings: 6

Cooking Time: 7 Minutes

Ingredients:

- 1½ pounds (680 g) unshelled edamame
- 2 tablespoons olive oil
- 1 teaspoon sea salt

Directions:

1. Place the edamame in a large bowl, then drizzle with olive oil. Toss to coat well. Transfer the edamame to the air fry basket.
2. Place the basket on the air fry position.
3. Select Air Fry, set temperature to 400ºF (205ºC) and set time to 7 minutes. Stir the edamame at least three times during cooking.
4. When done, the edamame will be tender and warmed through.
5. Transfer the cooked edamame onto a plate and sprinkle with salt. Toss to combine well and set aside for 3 minutes to infuse before serving.

Crispy Green Beans

Servings: 2 Cups
Cooking Time: 10 Minutes

Ingredients:

- ½ teaspoon lemon pepper
- 2 teaspoons granulated garlic
- ½ teaspoon salt
- 1 tablespoon olive oil
- 2 cups fresh green beans, trimmed and snapped in half

Directions:

1. Combine the garlic, lemon pepper, olive oil, and salt in a bowl. Stir to mix well.
2. Add the green beans to the bowl of mixture and toss to coat well.
3. Arrange the green beans in the air fry basket.
4. Place the basket on the bake position.
5. Select Bake, set temperature to 370ºF (188ºC) and set time to 10 minutes. Stir the green beans halfway through the cooking time.
6. When cooking is complete, the green beans will be tender and crispy. Remove from the air fryer grill.
7. Serve immediately.

Sweet And Spicy Peanuts

Servings: 9
Cooking Time: 5 Minutes

Ingredients:

- 3 cups shelled raw peanuts
- 1 tablespoon hot red pepper sauce
- 3 tablespoons granulated white sugar

Directions:

1. Put the peanuts in a large bowl, then drizzle with hot red pepper sauce and sprinkle with sugar. Toss to coat well.
2. Pour the peanuts in the air fry basket.
3. Place the basket on the air fry position.
4. Select Air Fry, set temperature to 400ºF (205ºC) and set time to 5 minutes. Stir the peanuts halfway through the cooking time.
5. When cooking is complete, the peanuts will be crispy and browned. Remove from the air fryer grill.
6. Serve immediately.

Hot Ham And Cheese Sandwich

Servings: 2
Cooking Time: 13 Minutes
Ingredients:

- 2-4 sandwich bread
- Olive oil
- 1/4 tsp. oregano & basil
- 4 ounces ham, sliced
- 4 ounces cheese, sliced

Directions:

1. Preheat the PowerXL Air Fryer Grill to 200ºC or 400ºF.
2. Apply olive oil and sprinkle oregano on both sides of bread slices.
3. Put the ham, spread cheese over one bread slice, and place the other on the sheet.
4. Bake for 10 minutes.

Nutrition Info: Calories: 245kcal, Carbs: 28g, Protein: 16.18g, Fat: 18.53g.

Crunchy Salty Tortilla Chips

Servings: 4
Cooking Time: 10 Minutes
Ingredients:

- 4 six-inch corn tortillas, cut in half and slice into thirds
- 1 tablespoon canola oil
- ¼ teaspoon kosher salt
- Cooking spray

Directions:

1. Spritz the air fry basket with cooking spray.
2. On a clean work surface, brush the tortilla chips with canola oil, then transfer the chips to the air fry basket.
3. Place the basket on the air fry position.
4. Select Air Fry, set temperature to 360ºF (182ºC) and set time to 10 minutes. Flip the chips and sprinkle with salt halfway through the cooking time.
5. When cooked, the chips will be crunchy and lightly browned. Transfer the chips to a plate lined with paper towels. Serve immediately.

Spicy-sweet Pork Tenderloin

Servings: 2 To 3

Cooking Time: 25 Minutes

Ingredients:

- 1 pound (454 g) pork tenderloin
- 2 tablespoons Sriracha hot sauce
- 2 tablespoons honey
- 1½ teaspoons kosher salt

Directions:

1. Stir together the honey, Sriracha hot sauce, and salt in a bowl. Rub the sauce all over the pork tenderloin.
2. Using the rotisserie spit, push through the pork tenderloin and attach the rotisserie forks.
3. If desired, place aluminum foil onto the drip pan. (It Servings: for easier clean-up!)
4. Place the prepared pork tenderloin with rotisserie spit into the air fryer grill.
5. Select Air Fry, set temperature to 350ºF (180ºC), Rotate, and set time to 20 minutes.
6. When cooking is complete, remove the pork tenderloin using the rotisserie lift and, using hot pads or gloves, carefully remove the chicken from the spit.
7. Let rest for 5 minutes and serve.

Air-fried Lemony Shishito Peppers

Servings: 4

Cooking Time: 5 Minutes

Ingredients:

- ½ pound (227 g) shishito peppers (about 24)
- 1 tablespoon olive oil
- Coarse sea salt, to taste
- Lemon wedges, for serving
- Cooking spray

Directions:

1. Spritz the air fry basket with cooking spray.
2. Toss the peppers with olive oil in a large bowl to coat well.
3. Arrange the peppers in the air fry basket.
4. Place the basket on the air fry position.
5. Select Air Fry, set temperature to 400ºF (205ºC) and set time to 5 minutes. Flip the peppers and sprinkle the peppers with salt halfway through the cooking time.
6. When cooked, the peppers should be blistered and lightly charred. Transfer the peppers onto a plate and squeeze the lemon wedges on top before serving.

Spicy Chicken Wings

Servings: 16 Wings
Cooking Time: 15 Minutes

Ingredients:

- 16 chicken wings
- 3 tablespoons hot sauce
- Cooking spray

Directions:

1. Spritz the air fry basket with cooking spray.
2. Arrange the chicken wings in the air fry basket.
3. Place the basket on the air fry position.
4. Select Air Fry, set temperature to 360ºF (182ºC) and set time to 15 minutes. Flip the wings at lease three times during cooking.
5. When cooking is complete, the chicken wings will be well browned. Remove the pan from the air fryer grill.
6. Transfer the air fried wings to a plate and serve with hot sauce.

Simple Air-fried Beef Roast

Servings: 6
Cooking Time: 38 Minutes

Ingredients:

- 2.5 pound (1.1 kg) beef roast
- 1 tablespoon olive oil
- 1 tablespoon Poultry seasoning

Directions:

1. Tie the beef roast and rub the olive oil all over the roast. Sprinkle with the seasoning.
2. Using the rotisserie spit, push through the beef roast and attach the rotisserie forks.
3. If desired, place aluminum foil onto the drip pan. (It Servings: for easier clean-up!)
4. Place the prepared chicken with rotisserie spit into the air fryer grill.
5. Select Air Fry. Set temperature to 360ºF (182ºC), and set time to 38 minutes for medium rare beef.
6. When cooking is complete, remove the beef roast using the rotisserie lift and, using hot pads or gloves, carefully remove the beef roast from the spit.
7. Let cool for 5 minutes before serving.

Fast Buttery Knots With Parsley

Servings: 8 Knots

Cooking Time: 5 Minutes

Ingredients:

- 1 teaspoon dried parsley
- ¼ cup melted butter
- 2 teaspoons garlic powder
- 1 (11-ounce / 312-g) tube refrigerated French bread dough, cut into 8 slices

Directions:

1. Combine the parsley, butter, and garlic powder in a bowl. Stir to mix well.
2. Place the French bread dough slices on a clean work surface, then roll each slice into a 6-inch long rope. Tie the ropes into knots and arrange them on a plate.
3. Transfer the knots into a baking pan. Brush the knots with butter mixture.
4. Slide the pan into the air fryer grill.
5. Select Air Fry, set temperature to 350ºF (180ºC) and set time to 5 minutes. Flip the knots halfway through the cooking time.
6. When done, the knots should be golden brown. Remove the pan from the air fryer grill.
7. Serve immediately.

Cheesy-creamy Broccoli Casserole

Servings: 6

Cooking Time: 30 Minutes

Ingredients:

- 4 cups broccoli florets
- ¼ cup heavy whipping cream
- ½ cup sharp Cheddar cheese, shredded
- ¼ cup ranch dressing
- Kosher salt and ground black pepper, to taste

Directions:

1. Combine all the ingredients in a large bowl. Toss to coat well broccoli well.
2. Pour the mixture into a baking pan.
3. Place the pan on the bake position.
4. Select Bake, set temperature to 375ºF (190ºC) and set time to 30 minutes.
5. When cooking is complete, the broccoli should be tender.
6. Remove the baking pan from the air fryer grill and serve immediately.

Golden Cheesy Potato Taquitos

Servings: 12 Taquitos

Cooking Time: 6 Minutes

Ingredients:

- 2 cups mashed potatoes
- ½ cup shredded Mexican cheese
- 12 corn tortillas
- Cooking spray

Directions:

1. Line a baking pan with parchment paper.
2. In a bowl, combine the cheese and potatoes until well mixed. Microwave the tortillas on high heat for 30 seconds, or until softened. Add some water to another bowl and set alongside.
3. On a clean work surface, lay the tortillas. Scoop 3 tablespoons of the potato mixture in the center of each tortilla. Roll up tightly and secure with toothpicks if necessary.
4. Arrange the filled tortillas, seam side down, in the prepared baking pan. Spritz the tortillas with cooking spray.
5. Place the pan into the air fryer grill.
6. Select Air Fry, set temperature to 400ºF (205ºC) and set time to 6 minutes. Flip the tortillas halfway through the cooking time.
7. When cooked, the tortillas should be crispy and golden brown.
8. Serve hot.

Standing Rib Roast

Servings: 8
Cooking Time: 90 Minutes
Ingredients:

- 5 lb. rib-eye meat
- Salt & pepper
- 1 tbsp. thyme
- 1 tbsp. rosemary
- 1 stick unsalted butter

Directions:

1. Preheat the PowerXL Air Fryer Grill to 230ºC or 450ºF.
2. Mix the butter and dry ingredients in a bowl.
3. Rub the mixture on the rib and roast it for an hour in the preheated PowerXL Air Fryer Grill.
4. Serve with fresh herbs on top.

Nutrition Info: Calories: 185kcal, Protein: 52.0 g, Fat: 48 g.

Burger Steak

Servings: 2
Cooking Time: 20 Minutes
Ingredients:

- 1 lb. ground beef
- 1 tablespoon parsley, chopped
- 1 onion, minced
- Salt and pepper to taste
- 1 cup mushroom gravy

Directions:

1. Mix ground beef, parsley, onion, salt and pepper in a bowl.
2. Form patties from the mixture.
3. Choose grill setting in the air fryer.
4. Set it to 375 degrees F.
5. Cook the burgers for 8 to 10 minutes per side.
6. Pour mushroom gravy on top and serve.

Baked White Rice

Servings: about 4 Cups

Cooking Time: 35 Minutes

Ingredients:

- 1 cup long-grain white rice, rinsed and drained
- 2 cups water
- 1 tablespoon unsalted butter, melted, or 1 tablespoon extra-virgin olive oil
- 1 teaspoon kosher salt or ½ teaspoon fine salt

Directions:

1. Add the butter and rice to the baking pan and stir to coat. Pour in the water and sprinkle with the salt. Stir until the salt is dissolved.
2. Place the pan on the bake position. Select Bake, set the temperature to 325ºF (163ºC), and set the time for 35 minutes.
3. After 20 minutes, remove the pan from the air fryer grill. Stir the rice. Transfer the pan back to the air fryer grill and continue cooking for 10 to 15 minutes, or until the rice is mostly cooked through and the water is absorbed.
4. When done, remove the pan from the air fryer grill and cover with aluminum foil. Let stand for 10 minutes. Using a fork, gently fluff the rice.
5. Serve immediately.

Crunchy Sweet Cinnamon Chickpeas

Servings: 2

Cooking Time: 10 Minutes

Ingredients:

- 1 tablespoon cinnamon
- 1 tablespoon sugar
- 1 cup chickpeas, soaked in water overnight, rinsed and drained

Directions:

1. Combine the cinnamon and sugar in a bowl. Stir to mix well.
2. Add the chickpeas to the bowl, then toss to coat well.
3. Pour the chickpeas in the air fry basket.
4. Place the basket on the air fry position.
5. Select Air Fry, set temperature to 390ºF (199ºC) and set time to 10 minutes. Stir the chickpeas three times during cooking.
6. When cooked, the chickpeas should be golden brown and crispy. Remove the basket from the air fryer grill.
7. Serve immediately.

Roast Beef

Servings: 6
Cooking Time: 30 Minutes

Ingredients:

- 4 lb. beef roast
- 1 tablespoon olive oil
- 1 teaspoon steak seasoning

Directions:

1. Drizzle roast with oil.
2. Sprinkle with steak seasoning.
3. Add to the air fryer.
4. Select rotisserie.
5. Cook at 360 degrees F for 50 minutes.

Crispy Brussels Sprouts

Servings: 4
Cooking Time: 20 Minutes

Ingredients:

- ¼ teaspoon salt
- ⅛ teaspoon ground black pepper
- 1 tablespoon extra-virgin olive oil
- 1 pound (454 g) Brussels sprouts, trimmed and halved
- Lemon wedges, for garnish

Directions:

1. Combine the olive oil, salt, and black pepper in a large bowl. Stir to mix well.
2. Add the Brussels sprouts to the bowl of mixture and toss to coat well. Arrange the Brussels sprouts in the air fry basket.
3. Place the basket on the air fry position.
4. Select Air Fry, set temperature to 350ºF (180ºC) and set time to 20 minutes. Stir the Brussels sprouts two times during cooking.
5. When cooked, the Brussels sprouts will be lightly browned and wilted. Remove from the air fryer grill.
6. Transfer the cooked Brussels sprouts to a large plate and squeeze the lemon wedges on top to serve.

Blistered Cherry Tomatoes

Servings: 4 To 6

Cooking Time: 10 Minutes

Ingredients:

- 2 pounds (907 g) cherry tomatoes
- 2 tablespoons olive oil
- 2 teaspoons balsamic vinegar
- ½ teaspoon salt
- ½ teaspoon ground black pepper

Directions:

1. Toss the cherry tomatoes with olive oil in a large bowl to coat well. Pour the tomatoes in a baking pan.
2. Slide the pan into the air fryer grill.
3. Select Air Fry, set temperature to 400ºF (205ºC) and set time to 10 minutes. Stir the tomatoes halfway through the cooking time.
4. When cooking is complete, the tomatoes will be blistered and lightly wilted.
5. Transfer the blistered tomatoes to a large bowl and toss with balsamic vinegar, salt, and black pepper before serving.

Crunchy Carrot

Servings: 2

Cooking Time: 18 Minutes

Ingredients:

- 1 tbsp of olive oil
- 4 carrots sliced
- 2 tsp of salt

Directions:

1. Mix the oil and salt in a bowl.
2. Pour the mixture on the carrot
3. Set the PowerXL Air Fryer Grill to air fry function.
4. Place the carrot mix on the PowerXL Air Fryer Grill pan.
5. Cook for 12 minutes at 360ºF.

Nutrition Info: Calories: 42kcal, Fat: 0.5g, Carb: 10g, Proteins: 1g

Fireless S'mores

Servings: 4

Cooking Time: 5 Minutes

Ingredients:

- 8 graham crackers
- 4 marshmallows
- 1 dark chocolate bar, chopped

Directions:

1. Put all the ingredients on top of the graham cracker and top with another cracker.
2. Roast it in the PowerXL Air Fryer Grill for 2 minutes.

Nutrition Info: Calories: 87kcal, Carbs: 6g, Protein: 01g, Fat: 03 g.

Creamy-cheesy Wontons

Servings: 4

Cooking Time: 6 Minutes

Ingredients:

- 2 ounces (57 g) cream cheese, softened
- 1 tablespoon sugar
- 16 square wonton wrappers
- Cooking spray

Directions:

1. Spritz the air fry basket with cooking spray.
2. In a mixing bowl, stir together the sugar and cream cheese until well mixed. Prepare a small bowl of water alongside.
3. On a clean work surface, lay the wonton wrappers. Scoop ¼ teaspoon of cream cheese in the center of each wonton wrapper. Dab the water over the wrapper edges. Fold each wonton wrapper diagonally in half over the filling to form a triangle.
4. Arrange the wontons in the basket. Spritz the wontons with cooking spray.
5. Place the basket on the air fry position.
6. Select Air Fry, set temperature to 350ºF (180ºC) and set time to 6 minutes. Flip the wontons halfway through the cooking time.
7. When cooking is complete, the wontons will be golden brown and crispy.
8. Divide the wontons among four plates. Let rest for 5 minutes before serving.

Crispy Kale Chips With Soy Sauce

Servings: 2
Cooking Time: 5 Minutes

Ingredients:

- 4 medium kale leaves, about 1 ounce (28 g) each, stems removed, tear the leaves in thirds
- 2 teaspoons soy sauce
- 2 teaspoons olive oil

Directions:

1. Toss the kale leaves with olive oil and soy sauce in a large bowl to coat well. Place the leaves in the baking pan.
2. Slide the pan into the air fryer grill.
3. Select Air Fry, set temperature to 400ºF (205ºC) and set time to 5 minutes. Flip the leaves with tongs gently halfway through.
4. When cooked, the kale leaves should be crispy. Remove the pan from the air fryer grill.
5. Serve immediately.

Classic French Fries

Servings: 2
Cooking Time: 25 Minutes

Ingredients:

- 2 russet potatoes, peeled and cut into ½-inch sticks
- 2 teaspoons olive oil
- Salt, to taste
- ¼ cup ketchup, for serving

Directions:

1. Bring a pot of salted water to a boil. Put the potato sticks into the pot and blanch for 4 minutes.
2. Rinse the potatoes under running cold water and pat dry with paper towels.
3. Put the potato sticks in a large bowl and drizzle with olive oil. Toss to coat well.
4. Transfer the potato sticks to the air fry basket.
5. Place the basket on the air fry position.
6. Select Air Fry, set temperature to 400ºF (205ºC) and set time to 25 minutes. Stir the potato sticks and sprinkle with salt halfway through.
7. When cooked, the potato sticks will be crispy and golden brown. Remove the French fries from the air fryer grill and serve with ketchup.

Roasted Pears

Servings: 3

Cooking Time: 60 Minutes

Ingredients:

- 3 semi-ripe pears
- 1/2 cup icing sugar
- 2 tbsp. butter
- 1 tbsp. ground cinnamon
- 3/4 cup white wine

Directions:

1. Mix all the ingredients, except for pears.
2. Prick the pears with a fork and let it soak in the wine mixture for 15 minutes.
3. Roast in the preheated PowerXL Air Fryer Grill for 20 minutes.

Nutrition Info: Calories: 103kcal, Carbs: 27g, Protein: 1g, Fat: 4g

Sausage Rolls

Servings: 16 Rolls

Cooking Time: 8 Minutes

Ingredients:

- 1 can refrigerated crescent roll dough
- 1 small package mini smoked sausages, patted dry
- 2 tablespoons melted butter
- 2 teaspoons sesame seeds
- 1 teaspoon onion powder

Directions:

1. Place the crescent roll dough on a clean work surface and separate into 8 pieces. Cut each piece in half and you will have 16 triangles.
2. Make the pigs in the blanket: Arrange each sausage on each dough triangle, then roll the sausages up.
3. Brush the pigs with melted butter and place of the pigs in the blanket in the air fry basket. Sprinkle with sesame seeds and onion powder.
4. Place the basket on the bake position.
5. Select Bake, set temperature to 330ºF (166ºC) and set time to 8 minutes. Flip the pigs halfway through the cooking time.
6. When cooking is complete, the pigs should be fluffy and golden brown.
7. Serve immediately.

Cheesy Wafer

Servings: 2

Cooking Time: 5 Minutes

Ingredients:

- 1 cup shredded aged Manchego cheese
- 1 teaspoon all-purpose flour
- ½ teaspoon cumin seeds
- ¼ teaspoon cracked black pepper

Directions:

1. Line the air fry basket with parchment paper.
2. Combine the cheese and flour in a bowl. Stir to mix well. Spread the mixture in the basket into a 4-inch round.
3. Combine the cumin and black pepper in a small bowl. Stir to mix well. Sprinkle the cumin mixture over the cheese round.
4. Place the basket on the air fry position.
5. Select Air Fry, set temperature to 375ºF (190ºC) and set time to 5 minutes.
6. When cooked, the cheese will be lightly browned and frothy.
7. Use tongs to transfer the cheese wafer onto a plate and slice to serve.

Golden Zucchini Sticks

Servings: 4

Cooking Time: 10 Minutes

Ingredients:

- 1 medium zucchini, cut into 48 sticks
- ¼ cup seasoned bread crumbs
- 1 tablespoon melted buttery spread
- Cooking spray

Directions:

1. Spritz the air fry basket with cooking spray and set aside.
2. In 2 different shallow bowls, add the seasoned bread crumbs and the buttery spread.
3. One by one, dredge the zucchini sticks into the buttery spread, then roll in the bread crumbs to coat evenly. Arrange the crusted sticks in the air fry basket.
4. Place the basket on the air fry position.
5. Select Air Fry, set temperature to 360ºF (182ºC) and set time to 10 minutes. Stir the sticks halfway through the cooking time.
6. When done, the sticks should be golden brown and crispy. Transfer the fries to a plate. Rest for 5 minutes and serve warm.

APPENDIX : RECIPES INDEX

www.ingramcontent.com/pod-product-compliance
Ingram Content Group UK Ltd.
Pitfield, Milton Keynes, MK11 3LW, UK
UKHW051132260726
13967UKWH00010B/3008